Vertamae Cooks

in

The Americas' Family Kitchen SM

Vertamae Cooks

in
The Americas'
Family Kitchen sm

Vertamae Grosvenor

Foreword by Ed Bradley

Food Photography by Joyce Oudkerk Pool

KQED BOOKS

San Francisco

For information, address:
KQED Books & Video, 2601 Mariposa St., San Francisco, CA 94110.

Publisher: James Connolly
Editorial Director: Pamela Byers
Managing Editor: Linda Brandt
Editor: Sharon Silva
Book Designer and Art Director: Traci Shiro and Richard Shiro
Illustrations: Richard Shiro
Food Photographer: Joyce Oudkerk Pool
Food Stylist: Pouké
Prop Stylist: Carol Hacker
Cover Portrait: Heimo
Food Stylist Assistant: Michelle Syracuse
Photo Assistant: Arjen Kammeraad
Special thanks to: Ethnic Arts and The Gardener, Berkeley, CA.

Book are available from KQED Books & Video for quantity purchases for sales promotions, premiums, fund-raising, or educational use. For more information, please write or call KQED Books & Video.

Grosvenor, Vertamae Smart
    Vertamae cooks in the Americas' family kitchen / Vertamae Grosvenor; foreword by Ed Bradley; food photography by Joyce Oudkerk Pool.
        p.   cm.
    "Companion to the Public Television series."
    Includes index.
    ISBN 0-912333-88-X (pbk.)
    1. Afro-American cookery. 2. Cookery, Caribbean. 3. Cookery, Latin America. 4. Cookery, African.   I. Title. II. Series: Americas' family kitchen (Television program)
TX715.S6377 1996
641.59'296073–dc20   96-42133
                                                                 CIP

ISBN 0-912333-88-x

Manufactured in Hong Kong
10 9 8 7 6 5 4 3 2 1

Distributed to the trade by Publishers Group West

On the back cover: Corn & Shrimp Chowder (page 37), Three-Onion Salsa (page 121), and Mommy's Quick Drop Peach Cobbler (page 170).

In Memoriam

Oscar Brown III
October 18, 1956 – August 12, 1996

About ten years ago, in an interview, painter and collagist Romare Bearden said an artist needs to find something, rescue it, and make it his or her own. That comment led me to conduct an exhaustive culinary folkloric investigation. The songs, stories, sayings, proverbs, jokes, riddles, and rhymes I found sang out like Fontella Bass, "Rescue Me." So I did. I started out with a performance piece, titled *Nyam*. Now the challenge...I needed to work with a musician...one in the tradition of Oscar Brown, Jr. Then, my daughter Chandra married Oscar Brown III. Bo, as he was called, collaborated with me on songs for *Nyam*. Bo was a gifted musician. *That boy could play the bass–you hear me!* And he was sho nuff in the tradition. He would hum, pat the hambone, jig on juba dis' and juba dat', hollar out vendor calls and work those plantation ditties, *Boil dem Cabbage Down, Peas and Rice* and *Carve dat Possum*. Bo could "rescue" a song from any conversation or situation. I came across the old timey courtship line, "Sir, you are a huckleberry beyond my persimmon. Bo said, "Yeah, Mom, that's a song. Write the words, I got the music." This summer, on Juneteenth, we played our last gig In Kansas City. In a barbecue joint, we observed the very unique cultural culinary dialogue as each customer ordered. Their bebop blues exchange inspired a song. Bo said, "Mom, write the words, I got the music."

Yeah Bo, I got the words for the song but none to say how I miss you...you huckleberry beyond my persimmon.

Bo's Notes

One thing I've learned from
    playing wrong notes
Is that there are
None.
Notes are choices
Occurring in space
And time and renew
Into the next
Ever changing notes
Of infinity
Notes leading to
Descending from note
Notes ask the questions
The next note will answer
Notes generating, creating notes
Within notes
All notes in all notes
I've lived in pursuit
Of the most precious
Notes my soul has
Known
Ageless note that thru
Time still rings

    Oscar Brown III
    August 11, 1996

*The four O's:
Oscar Brown, Jr.;
Oscar III holding Little O, Oscar IV;
Big O, Oscar Brown. 1988.*

Foreword

Verta Mae Grosvenor is a charmer. That she's also a great cook is not the least of her charms. I have known Verta for almost thirty years, although I almost didn't get to know her. You see, I met her daughters first. Marie Brown, a mutual friend, brought Verta's children, Kali and Chandra, to my apartment in New York. At the time they were five and seven years old. Some would call them cute, others precocious. I didn't know what to make of them. I just knew I'd never seen any kids act quite like these two. After a few hours, I gave Marie five dollars to take them home in a taxi (it was that long ago). Eventually, I got to know them, and I grew to love them. Obviously, charm runs in the family.

Back in the day—that would be in the sixties— when New York was awash in antiwar protests, school decentralization battles that often took place in the streets, and assorted movement issues, Verta's home on the lower East Side was a convenient stopping point for me on my daily rounds as a reporter for one of the local radio stations. It was close to City Hall, not far from the Brooklyn Bridge, the FDR Drive, and just off of Houston Street. Not only was it convenient, but if you timed it right, there might be a pot on the stove. And, a pot on Verta's stove is something special.

We've had our differences over the years. I think everyone who knows Verta has. But we all come back. It's her charm. And nowhere is she more charming than in the kitchen. I've had days when Verta got rid of me but allowed me to come back for supper.

Once, when I was living in Paris, she breezed through town as only she can. I had told everyone about her prowess in the kitchen so we were anxiously awaiting a Verta Mae home-cooked meal. We went shopping on Strasbourg-St. Denis. And I began to get a little nervous. Verta is from the school of cooks who make up their mind when they see what is in the market. She may shop with a few ideas in her head but she definitely has to survey everything just to see what they have. Besides, it had been some years since she'd been to Paris and I suspected she wanted to take her time.

I'm a little different. I go with a menu in mind and a backup menu or two in case they don't have my first choice. I move quickly and purposefully. Verta dawdles. Or as she would say, "Edward, I like to savor the experience". Well, we walked from one end of Strasbourg-St. Denis to the other checking all the stores for meat, fish, cheese, pastries, vegetables. "I think the fish looks better here, Edward." "Great, Verta, let's buy it." But to my chagrin we bought nothing. Then we started back up the other side of the street doing the same thing.

By the time we got back to where we started, my patience was fading fast. When she bought some vegetables I had never seen before, I wondered aloud what she was doing. But when she bought the chicken, I went over the edge. Now, I'd been raised on fried chicken and Verta cooks chicken with the best of them. But did she buy a whole chicken? No. Did she buy cut- up parts? No. She bought the feet. Not the legs, the feet. At that point, I saw everyone coming to dinner for some kind of weird dish with the unknown vegetable and chicken feet. My patience was up and so was hers. She said, "Edward, go home. Just leave me alone."

So, off I went, wondering what would be in store for dinner. I shouldn't have worried. Verta had pulled something out of her culinary bag of tricks that utilized this odd vegetable (I still don't know what it was) and the chicken feet as a seasoning. My friends in Paris were knocked out by the meal.

Throughout this cookbook, Verta Mae brings you her charm and a world of culinary know-how. Each recipe comes with a story and is blended with all of the special ingredients she shares from experience. I know this book will enable you to charm your friends and family, and feed them very well.

Ed Bradley
CBS NEWS

 Acknowledgments

KQED Books gave me a lot of space for acknowledgments. Even so, it's not enough for all the names of everyone I want and need to thank. So for those whose names are not here, I want you to know that I hold you in my memory and my heart.

I especially want to thank Fran Harth, Executive Producer of *The Americas' Family Kitchen*, for giving me the opportunity to cook on television and to share my ideas about Afro-Atlantic cooking.

I am grateful to Director Tim Ward; Producer Beverly Price; Katherine Lauderdale; Ron Nigro; *The Americas' Family Kitchen* technical crew; makeup artist Aimee Tolson, who tried to make me look good and always lifted my spirits; and everyone at WTTW for their guidance and patience as I learned that cooking on a kitchen set ain't like cooking in a kitchen.

Thanks to Ann Robinson and everyone at PBS for understanding and supporting the series.

Special thanks to my attorney, Amy Goldson, for her brilliant counsel; my colleagues at National Public Radio for their support, and Sharon Green and Bill Busenberg for allowing me to juggle time so that I could work on this project. Thanks to my home girls, Sandra Rattley-Lewis and Mary Beth Kirschner, who put *seasoning* in my life, and the Frugal Gourmet, Jeff Smith, for coming by the set and giving me his blessing on the first day of taping.

I am *very* grateful to everyone at KQED Books for their hard and very fine work. My deepest appreciation goes to Editorial Director Pam Byers, Managing Editor Linda Brandt, and Designers Traci and Rich Shiro, for believing in this book and helping it take shape. Heimo made me look good on the cover, and Photographer Joyce Oudkerk Pool with stylists Pouké and Carol Hacker made pictures as good as my food. And most heartfelt thanks to Editor Sharon Silva for her skillful editing and organizing.

And now I want to thank all my people, past and present, public and private, who added a pinch, a dash, and a potful of time, advice, recipes, stories, love and laughter to my personal culinary history.

First, the Penn Center on St. Helena Island and its Director, Emory Campbell, for their enduring support. *The Americas' Family Kitchen* owes one to Emma Campbell, who drove six miles each way in search of cowpeas to Fed Ex for the "Hoppin' John" show! And to Jeanne and Arthur Ashe for those good times on St. Helena and good fish *samiches*.

Thanks to the only person I know who dresses to cook, Josephine Premice, for introducing me to Paul Winfield, who took time to literally find a recipe amid his kitchen renovations. Thanks to Calvin Lockhart who introduced me to Josephine. Although he didn't give me a recipe for this book, he remains a culinary inspiration. Thanks to LeRoy Henderson for the Muhammad Ali photo, and to Edward Bradley, who managed to write the foreword and still cover the political conventions. Thanks to Marie Dutton Brown for introducing me to Edward, and David Jackson, who turned going to the store into a high art form.

Thanks Hart Leroy Bibbs, Patrick Letiller, Quincy Troupe, Margaret Porter, Hugh Masekela, David Murray, David Perry, Julie Dash, Junette Pinkney, Cheryl Woodruff, Beverly Robinson, Jennifer Richards, Jonathan Green, Hoppin' John Taylor, Bob Tucker (hello Miz Inez), Sue Goodwin, Terrell Lamb, Emillio and Pat Cruz, Lucille Clifton, Corrine Jennings, Joe Overstreet, George and T., Amina and Amira Baraka, Eleanor Traylor, James Haskins, Daisy Voight, Leslie Peters, Charles Jefferies, Paula Carlotti, Toni Cade Bambara, The Johnson Girls and the Blue Plate Special, Bill Gunn, Damon Lee Fowler, Rosemarie Ritter, and Vanessea Niles.

Thank you to the staff at Lenox Suites in Chicago and the adjacent Andrews Restaurant, especially Flora. To the folks at the Washington D.C. Columbia Road Safeway, who wished me well on the project after they found out I was buying food to test recipes every day, not because I had a ferocious appetite. Thanks to Ricardo Mondadori, who, from the first time I mentioned the idea of Afro-Atlantic cookery, said: "What a delicious idea." And Gullah woman Dr. Rowena Stuart, who was Director of the Afro-American Museum, where we did the first performances of *Nyam*, and is now Director of the 18th and Vine Authority where we gave the last.

And a basketful of warm hugs to my family, the Ritters and the Smarts, who in the most difficult hours of the project, when the pots were on the back burner, said "Don't out the fire, keep on cooking." Thanks to my daughters, Chandra, for her invaluable research and typing, and Kali, whose educated palate served as "food critic."

And all this wouldn't be possible without the love of my godson, Porter Troupe, and my grandchildren, Oscar Brown IV and Charlotte Rose Grosvenor Jefferies, who show promise of becoming the first great chefs of the 21st century.

Vertamae Grosvenor

t a b l e   o f

Watermelon Soup • Virginia-style Goober Soup • Sunshine Soup • Caribbean Pumpkin Soup with Beef Short Ribs • Chandra's Cuban-style Black Bean Soup • Philly Pepperpot Soup • Caribbean Pepperpot Soup • Corn & Shrimp Chowder • Caribbean Congo Pea Soup • Creek Indian Pepperpot Soup • Brazilian Palm Heart Soup

Summertime Three-Melon Salad • Apple & Pear Salad • Southern Pasta & Bean Salad • Black-eyed Pea Salad • Peanut Waldorf Salad • Old-fashioned Coleslaw • Fresh Beet Salad • Palm Hearts & Beet Salad • Classic White Potato Salad • Tropical Sweet Potato Salad • White & Wild Rice Salad

Broiled Fish with Peanut Salsa • Mullet Stew • Low Country Broiled Fish • Baked Bass with Vegetables • Fried Catfish • Ackee & Saltfish • Saltfish Fritters • Daufuskie Island Deviled Crab • Shrimp & Goobers • Bahian Shrimp Stew • South Carolina Shrimp Perlou • Shrimp Creole • Shrimp & Sausage Gumbo • Jollof Rice • Jerk Chicken • Arroz con Pollo • Bobby Seale's Spicy Chicken Barbecue • Groundnut Stew • Oven-fried Lemon Chicken Wings • Braised Guinea Hen • Jambalaya • Crown Pork Roast with Sage-Apple Cornbread Stuffing • Auntie Kali's Puerto Rican-style Pork Roast • Barbecued Beef Brisket with Dry Rub • Jamaican Curried Goat • Limpin' Susan • Hoppin' John • Gullah Vegetable Paella • Saint Helena Stew • Vegetable Gumbo

Contents

The Beginning Tale

This unprecedented culinary tale began centuries ago in the land of cassava, cowrie shells, calabashes, ivory, gold, and wild watermelons.

In this place the seas were full of scale and shell fish, the forests were abundant with large and small game. Here were kola and groundnuts, grape and breadfruits, sweet and soursops, spices of every kind, and a dizzying array of greens, including a spinach said to make a husband robust and fresh.

Benne seeds, what we call sesame seeds, were bearers of good luck, and the baobab tree was righteous. Its vitamin-rich leaves were cooked, the flesh of its fruit eaten raw, its seeds made into tea or placed under the tongue to quench thirst, and its hollowed trunk fashioned into a hut.

Pepper was the staff of life. Indeed, it was the spice of the land. The west coast was called the Pepper Coast in honor of the grains of paradise. A popular proverb said, "The man who eats no pepper is weak."

"The king is not on his stool."

"The queen is gone."

"The warrior is gone."

"The dancer is gone."

"The holy man is vanished."

This was a land of man gods . . . kingdoms, queens, warriors, weavers, and workers of magic. Night was the only winter the people knew, and the sound of the drum was always heard.

The people made art, sang praisesongs, offered food to their ancestors, drank palm wine, and sang songs of praise to such a splendid homeland.

And then a pillage was upon them! In villages throughout the land, people came up missing.

A young bride went to fill her calabash with water and didn't return.

Imagine an Ashanti bride cooking rice in Kingston. Imagine a thirsty Yoruba king in a Cuban canebrake. Imagine a kidnapped Dahomey queen in the kitchen of Mount Vernon, a Senegambian prince preparing she-crab soup in Charleston.

Imagine a Hausa holy man, a Muslim, serving ham at Monticello, a Mandinka drummer stirring mint juleps in Kentucky, a Guinea dancer in the cookhouse of Tuckahoe Plantation on the James River in Virginia.

Who knows what was on the mind of the dancer racing food along the batter express, the path leading from the cookhouse to the big house. Who knows what was on the mind of the Hausa holy man.

In the land of the magnolias, a place with no palm oil and no drums, the Africans, like the Israelites in the wilderness, had a longing for the foods of their homeland.

While some of the foods in the New World were familiar and similar, there were tastes and smells the Africans would never know again.

Perhaps that is why every time she took the benne seed cakes, the seeds of good luck, from the oven, the Dahomey queen fumbled.

Island woman.
Postcard from the Penn Center
St. Helena, South Carolina.

Introduction

Do you believe that hundreds and hundreds of Africans brought here on this other side would forget everything they once knew?
Nana Pazant, *Daughters of the Dust*

vertamae 1960

"E teif me pinders n e hand een ain onrabel e mout!"

"What? I don't understand a word you are saying! Speak English!"

"E teif me pinders, me goobers them, n e take he foot n e hand een ain onrabel e mout!"

"I said speak English!"

"She can't speak no English teacher. She is one of those bad-talking rice eating Geechees from South Carolina."

Laughter.

The laughter hurt my ten-year-old heart and brought tears to my eyes. I longed to be back in the South Carolina Low Country, where eating rice wasn't funny and the teacher would understand when I said a boy stole my peanuts and ran off without saying a word.

We descendants of African slaves in the Low Country have intrigued scholars and anthropologists for more than a century. They call us Gullah, but "we called weself Geechee." We say goober or pinder for peanut, gombo for okra, and benne for sesame seed. Buckra means white and can be a white potato or a white person. A skillet blond is a very dark person. We say guinea squash for eggplant and nyam for to eat. I didn't know that people in the rest of the country – or even in the rest of the state – spoke differently from us until I left the Low Country to go north. Geechee territory was my home.

lettuce field

Home was where there was always a pot of rice on the stove or in the icebox. If you asked, "What you having for dinnah?" nobody mentioned rice. That was a given.

Home was where everybody worked in the field. Lord, I hated field work. I once feigned sunstroke by eating a bar of soap and rubbing Watkin's linament on my body, and then "falling out" in the yard. I had "my attack" after the midday meal while everyone was sitting on the front porch waiting for the sun to drop closer to the horizon so they could return to the fields. I writhed on the ground in front of them, frothing at the mouth and moaning "sunstroke, sunstroke." A cousin had seen me with the soap and linament and tried to tell them I was faking. But she was what used to be called tongue-tied, and since I was the only person who could understand her, she couldn't tattle on me.

I was never sure if Grandmama Sula was fooled or not, but from then on I didn't have to go back to the fields. I stayed at the house and helped with the cooking. I gathered eggs from the henhouse, vegetables from the garden, prepared food without running water, and cooked on a wood-burning stove. It was hard work, but these were glory days when compared to the fields.

I learned how to "turn around in the kitchen": when to cook corn bread so it arrives hot at the table, when to put the peas on the back burner, how to clean a chicken gizzard, how to crack an egg without breaking the yolk. But I could not break the code of Gullah kitchen talk. The women talked as they shelled peas and cut greens, but their conversations were like puzzles.

"If you want your milk sweet, leave it in the cow."
"A turnip top don't tell the size of the turnip."
"You right about that!"
"There's salt in the sweet bread."
"A most kill bird don't make soup."
"Her tongue don't know no Sunday."
"Hope is a good breakfast but a bad supper."
"Uhh uhh!"
"God don't eat okra."
"You can say that again."
"God don't eat okra."

Islander grinding corn

Man and boy

Photograph by Leigh Richmond Minor, circa 1900 (postcards from the Penn Center St. Helena Island, South Carolina)

Home was where "yenna come nyan" meant "come and eat." I didn't know that nyam was an African root word used throughout the diaspora. I didn't know there were cultural reasons why we were big rice eaters, that there were African retentions in the way Grandmama Sula made okra soup, in the way Granddaddy made baskets, or in the way Mr. Knowels cast his net in the river. What did I know from African retentions or diaspora?

I had heard some talk of "salt-water Africans" and of slaves in the field who would grab a magic hoe and fly back to Africa. Mother Dear, my other grandmother, said one of her grandmother's favorite expressions was "If I don't see you no more, I'll see you in Aficky." But I didn't think that all of that had something to do with food.

I was a grown girl and across the ocean before I, as folklorist Zora Neale Hurston has described it, looked at home through the spyglass of anthropology and began my exploration into Afro-Atlantic food ways.

It has been an exciting journey. Much of our culinary past is lost history, however, and it seems that the more that is known, the more questions are raised. In the 1960s and 1970s, when everyone was searching for his or her roots, one of the major cultural finds was Black American culinary heritage. I thought that finally we would have the flavor of Africa in the melting pot and that we would appreciate and celebrate it. "Soul food" got hot, but it was a passing thing. Folks went on believing that black cookery was a highly seasoned food group of bones and lard, created from "massa's leftovers," and people, including many soul food eaters, swallowed that tidbit of culinary history.

*Grandmama Gula Ritter
Some cousins
My father, Frank Smart,
taken 1952.
He could cook the black
off a skillet and the white
off of rice.*

*Uncle Zander,
who was a great cook,
Aunt Vister, a cousin*

cover of old Creole cookbook

Me, in 1951

Although most people now acknowledge that black hands stirred the pots of early America, there is still much to learn, for African-American cookery is an intricate mosaic. It's owning a cast-iron skillet and a Cuisinart. It's as classic as iced tea, as zesty as ginger beer, and as elementary as lemonade. It's as old as gumbo and as new as a collard greens soufflé. It's sweet potato biscuits, piping-hot hush puppies, turnip tops with cornmeal dumplings, creamy rice pudding, and a hoecake cooked on a hoe in the cotton field.

It's the seasoning that fur trader Jim Pierce used in his beaver tail ragouts. It's butter churned on the dashing of a covered wagon on the westward trek. It's hot gumbos and cold aspics on Mississippi steamboats.

And it's still more: A fried chicken and white bread sandwich in a shoebox on the train up north. A bowl of clabber and corn bread from a neighbor when you are too poor to buy a waltzing jacket for a flea. A glass of homemade dandelion wine when your niece, the first in your family, graduates from college. A pan of Aunt Zipporah's macaroni and cheese at uncle Bubba's wake. A batch of Cousin Ruby's rolls at the family reunion.

Afro-Atlantic cookery is as comical as the rooster and the chicken in the hen house.

The rooster and the chicken had a fight

The chicken knocked the rooster outta sight

The rooster told the chicken "Dats alrite,

I'll meet you in the gumbo tomorrow night!"

This cookery is sometimes a riddle.

What's sweet water standing up?
    Answer: sugarcane.

What goes up white and comes down yellow?
    Answer: an egg.

What goes up green and comes down red?
    Answer: a watermelon.

What has one hundred windows and no doors?
    Answer: a fishnet.

What's a black hen sitting on a red hen's nest?
    Answer: a black cast-iron pot on the fire.

Oscar Brown Jr and Oscar III
Photo: Bob Hsiang

And this cookery is sometimes a dream.

To dream of salt signifies disgrace and remorse.

To dream of eating rice denotes riches.

To dream of onions means you will lose your mind.

To dream of pork chops indicates sickness.

To dream of sweet potatoes means you will meet the person of your dreams.

To dream of white potatoes foretells an unhappy marriage.

To dream of fish means somebody in your family is pregnant.

To dream of sausages portends you will outwit your enemies and be happy.

Howard Myers
(Estellas brother)

Outside the red house on family homestead with cousins. Bouquet of flowers from Grandmama Sula's old garden.

But the borders of Afro-Atlantic cookery reach beyond a pot of rice on a supper table in the South Carolina Low Country or a gumbo in a tureen in an old-fashioned New Orleans diner. The culinary legacy of Africa in the Americas is also a moqueca in Bahia, a plate of moros y cristianos in Havana, a dish of curried goat in Kingston. It's wherever slave traders transported millions of Africans to in the New World. It's the kitchens of sugar plantations in Cuba and Jamaica, of coffee and cacao plantations in Brazil.

My explorations into the food customs and connections of the Afro-Atlantic community have filled a scrapbook with snapshots, recipes, menus, and drawings. It holds archival pictures of cane workers in Cuba, photographs of a woman grinding corn on Saint Helena Island, and brochures of the Festival of the Cooks on Guadeloupe. There are stanzas of Sarah Webster Fabio's "Don't Mess with My Fungi," the words to such spirituals as "Lord, Don't Let this Harvest Pass," and Robert Johnson's blues line "You betta come on in my kitchen."

Edward Bradley and Marie Brown in the 70's

During my journey, I have added new words to my culinary vocabulary— vatapa, mondongo, griots, roti, bocaditos, calaloo—and have collected cookbooks from everywhere in the Americas. My most treasured of these is Comidas Criollas Peruanas given to me over two decades ago by my dear friend photographer Robert Fletcher. I had talked to him so much about *"the flavor of Africa throughout the Americas, that when Bob was on assignment in Peru and saw the book with a black woman who resembled Aunt Jemima on the cover, he brought it back to me.*

My National Public Radio show, "Seasonings," has given me the opportunity to meet and talk with great cooks, from Zydeco Queen Ida to a mole expert in central Mexico to Graceland's Mary Jenkins, who shared Elvis's favorite recipes. In North Carolina, I sat in a kitchen with celebrated poet and great cook, Maya Angelou, and in South Carolina I listened to master cook Katherine Austin relate the tale of a three-legged chicken and talk about cush-cush, an old-timey American dish with African roots.

Talking with Muhammad Ali at training camp 1974 Photo: LeRoy W. Henderson

Cooking with young cooks in the 70's in NYC

Emory Campbell at Penn Center St. Helena Island, South Carolina

SOUTH CAROLINA

PENN SCHOOL
One of the first schools for blacks in the South, Penn School, opened in 1862, was reorganized as Penn Normal, Industrial and Agricultural School in 1901. As a result of this change, incorporating principles of education found at both Tuskegee and Hampton institutes, Penn became an international model. Its program was removed to the Beaufort County school system in 1948.

On location shooting
The Americas' Family Kitchen

Photograph by Dave Moyer

In the studio

I continued my journey on Public Television's "The Americas' Family Kitchen." I traveled to Jamaica where I ate a sumptuous meal prepared by cookbook author Enid Donaldson and took a ride on the wild side up the Blue Mountains to a coffee plantation. Back home, pitmaster Bobby Seale, who doesn't believe in barbecue secrets, divulged to me that he had learned as a boy in Texas. The series also gave me the chance to do what I love most: cook with my family. On the "Sunday Supper" show, my granddaughter, Charlotte Rose, made corn bread and helped me clean the greens, while my grandson, Oscar, baked Brown sugar cookies.

My family is a cooking family, men and women alike. After "Hello, how are you?" the next words out of their mouths are "Let's cook!" No matter how different our lifestyles or our politics, we all get along in the kitchen. We are a family of adventurous palates, too, always ready to try both new dishes and new seasonings for old favorites. There might even be chicken prepared in a couple of different ways at the same meal, because one person wanted to fix it like they had it in Senegal, and someone else wanted to make it the way it's done in Costa Rica.

And that is the spirit of this book—openness to new tastes and new seasonings. Afro-Atlantic cookery is a rich heritage born out of a great diaspora. I hope that "Vertamae Cooks In The Americas' Family Kitchen" will be your guide to that vast culinary world. I'm still on my journey, learning, eating, and cooking. But I've set a place for you now, so you'd betta come on in to my kitchen.

Glossary

Ackee Red, pear-shaped fruit with yellow flesh the color of scrambled eggs; commonly combined with saltfish in Jamaica.

Beet Greens Flavorful green leaves with red stems and veins cut from the tops of beets. Also known as beet tops.

Black Beans Small dried black beans regularly used in Brazilian and Caribbean cuisines.

Black-eyed Peas Type of cowpea with a creamy color and a distinctive black "eye" at its center. Widely available dried.

Breadfruit Large vegetable fruit, with flesh commonly roasted and served as a vegetable.

Calabaza A large cousin of the American pumpkin with yellow flesh and a yellow-green exterior.

Carver, Dr. George Washington Famed African-American agricultural chemist, research scientist, and educator who developed hundreds of uses for the peanut and the sweet potato, as well as other crops.

Cassava Also known as yuca and manioc. Native to Brazil, a long, starchy tuber native with white flesh. Cooked much like a potato as well as ground for flour.

Catfish Firm, meaty fish with a whiskered face; widely farmed in the South.

Collard Greens Member of the cabbage family with large, deep green leaves and an assertive flavor.

Congo Peas Also known as pigeon peas or gungo peas. Native to Africa, beige beans with red mottling; most often found dried.

Couve Brazilian dish of sauteed shredded kale (see page 129).

Cowpeas Also known as field peas or crowder peas. Close relative of the black-eyed pea, with an earthy flavor and creamy color. Most often found dried, but occasionally available fresh.

Crab Boil A packaged mixture of herbs and spices—mustard seeds, bay leaves, cayenne pepper, dill, and so on—for adding to the boiling water in which crab, lobster, or other shellfish are cooked.

Creole Cooking Famed in the South; a blend of Spanish, African, French, and West Indian influences in which such ingredients as okra, tomatoes, peppers, and rice play major roles.

Daufuskie Island One of South Carolina's Sea Islands, and the only one of the islands not connected to the mainland by a bridge.

Dende Oil Red-orange cooking oil extracted from the fruit of a native West African palm; commonly used in Brazilian cooking.

File Powder Ground young leaves of the sassafras tree, used for thickening soups and stews.

Fritter Batter generally containing vegetables, fruits, or other foods sauteed or deep fried.

Fungi Caribbean dish that combines cornmeal and okra (see page 128).

Geechee Dialect word for Gullah.

Goober Southern name for the peanut.

Groundnut Name for the peanut, used primarily in Britain and its former colonies.

Guinea Hen Also called guinea fowl. West African native, related to the pheasant, with tender, lean flesh and a pleasantly gamey flavor.

Gullah A descendant of African slaves from the coastal areas of South Carolina, Georgia, and the tip of northeastern Florida; also, the language spoken by these people.

Gumbo Southern stew traditionally composed of a variety of vegetables and chicken, seafood, and/or sausage, thickened with okra or file powder and served over rice. Also, another name for okra.

Ham Hock Upper part of the foreleg of the pig, usually sold smoked.

Hoecake A small, savory cornmeal cake fried in a skillet (see page 155).

Hominy Grits The dried kernels of field corn that have been hulled and coarsely cracked; available in regular, quick-cooking, and instant forms.

Hoppin' John Southern dish comprised of cowpeas or black-eyed peas, rice, and usually bacon, salt pork, or sausages (see page 102).

Hush Puppies Cornmeal batter shaped into cakes and fried in hot fat (see page 142).

Jambalaya Southern dish that traditionally combines rice with chicken, ham, sausages, and sometimes tomatoes (see page 93).

Jerk Name given to Jamaican dishes in which a fiery mix of spices--the jerk rub--is used to season poultry and meats that are then cooked over an open fire.

Johnny Cake A bread made of cornmeal and water or milk either baked in a pan in the oven or deep-fried (see page 157).

Jollof Rice West African rice dish of meats, seafood, and vegetables that varies according to what is on hand (see page 83).

Kale Member of the cabbage family with dark green, ruffle-edged leaves; a favorite of Brazilian cooks.

Limpin' Susan Southern dish of rice, shrimp, and okra (see page 101).

Liquid Smoke Commercial product that imparts a smoky flavor to grilled foods.

Low Country The coastal areas of Southern states.

Manioc See cassava.

Moros y Cristianos Literally, "Moors and Christians"; popular Cuban dish of black beans cooked with rice (see page 132).

Mullet Mild white-fleshed fish found in along the coast of the Carolinas south to Florida.

Okra Native to Africa, slender, slightly fuzzy green pods that have a mucilaginous quality when cooked, making them excellent thickeners for soups and stews.

Paella A saffron-flavored Spanish rice dish that usually includes seafood, poultry, and vegetables.

Palm Heart The heart of a variety of palm tree; popular ingredient in Brazilian cuisine and in some cuisines of the South.

Pepperpot A soup or stew of vegetables, meats or fish, and seasonings common in the West Indies and in some parts of the United States.

Pepper Vinegar Southern condiment of distilled white vinegar and fiery chilies.

Perlou The signature rice dish of South Carolina, which mixes rice with seafood, meats, and/or vegetables (see page 77).

Pone Word used to describe variously a bread, pudding, or side dish made from corn or sweet potatoes, often served as a savory and sometimes as a sweet.

Ratatouille Name for a French Provencal dish that combines tomatoes, peppers, zucchini, eggplant, and seasonings, as well as dishes similar to it (see page 126).

Red Beans Name commonly used for dried red kidney beans.

Saffron Fragrant, golden orange spice made from the dried stigmas of a crocus flower.

Saint Helena Island One of the South Carolina Sea Islands, and site of the first school for freed blacks in the South.

Saltfish Term used in the Caribbean, particularly in Jamaica, for salted cod.

Salt Pork Salt-cured bacon comprised mostly of pork fat with a few streaks of meat.

Soul Food Popular term for African-American cuisine.

Succotash Mixture of lima beans and corn cooked together, sometimes with other ingredients (see page 130).

Swamp Cabbage Name popularly used for palm hearts in the South.

Sweet Potato Tuberous root member of the morning glory family with yellow flesh and brownish skin.

Tripe The muscular lining of the stomach of cows and other ruminants.

Turnip Greens Smooth, flat green leaves clipped from the tops of turnips.

Wild Rice An aquatic grass with long, dark brown grains; no botanical relation to rice.

Yam Term used in the United States for a variety of sweet potato with orange flesh and deep purple or brownish skin.

Yam, African A mealy-textured tuberous root, unrelated to the common American yam, with brownish or yellowish skin, yellow or white flesh, and a mild potato flavor.

Yuca See cassava.

Soups

Because it is slightly sweet, a watermelon soup does not have a fixed place in a meal. It is, of course, a natural dish in the heat of summer, but should this delicate soup be served before or after the main course? I suggest you put it out on a buffet table. That way, your guests can eat it whenever they want.

Watermelon Soup

½ cup sugar

2 cups water

1 piece watermelon, about 2 pounds

1 or 2 lemons

1 cup heavy cream

Fresh mint leaves

In a small, heavy saucepan, combine the sugar and water and bring to a simmer, stirring constantly to dissolve the sugar. Cook over low heat, stirring occasionally, for about 5 minutes until a light syrup forms. Remove from the heat and let cool.

Using a large spoon, scoop out the flesh from the watermelon. Pick over and discard any seeds.

Working in batches, in a blender or a food processor, liquefy the melon flesh while gradually adding the cooled syrup. Transfer to a bowl. Add the cream to the bowl and stir well. Squeeze the juice from the lemons and add to taste. Stir well, cover, and chill.

To serve, ladle into bowls and garnish with mint.

Serves 6

Watermelon Etiquette I had the shock of my life the first time I was in Europe and saw people eating watermelon with a knife and fork. I was used to "busting" melons and sticking my face right up into the heart of the fruit. For that reason, I could never order watermelon in a restaurant – not because I was ashamed, of course, but because I simply couldn't bring myself to use a knife and fork to eat it.

During the colonial era, peanut soup was popular, particularly in Virginia. People who visited there went home talking about the delicious goober soup. If there was a piece of pork or beef in the smokehouse, it would go into the pot first, for extra flavor.

Virginia-style Goober Soup

Chop the onion and peel and dice the carrots.

In a heavy saucepan over medium heat, melt the butter. Add the onion and carrots and saute until the vegetables begin to soften, about 5 minutes. Add 1 cup of the chicken stock, reduce the heat to low, and simmer, uncovered, until the vegetables are softened, about 15 minutes. Remove from the heat and let cool for a few minutes.

Working in batches if necessary, combine the vegetables and their cooking liquid, the peanut butter, and 1 cup of the chicken stock in a food processor fitted with the metal blade. Process until smooth.

Transfer the pureé to the saucepan and add the rice, salt, black and cayenne peppers, and the remaining 2 cups chicken stock. Place over low heat and bring to a simmer. Cover and simmer gently, stirring occasionally, until heated through and the flavors are blended, about 10 minutes. Ladle into bowls to serve.

Serves 4 to 6

1 yellow onion

2 carrots

3 tablespoons butter

4 cups chicken stock

1 cup unsalted smooth peanut butter

½ cup cooked white rice

Salt, ground black pepper, and cayenne pepper to taste

Boiled Peanuts Alongside the roadways on the coast of South Carolina, there are stands selling boiled peanuts. These are young peanuts that are boiled in water until they take on a wonderful deep flavor and slightly crumbly texture. They are definitely an acquired taste, but people who like them become addicts. Whenever I go home to South Carolina, friends up North press me to bring some back.

This Caribbean soup is the color of a tropical sun. Any yellow or golden winter squash—acorn, Hubbard, or butternut—can be substituted for the calabaza.

Sunshine Soup

1 piece calabaza, about 2 pounds

1 large yellow onion

2 cloves garlic

2 tomatoes

2 tablespoons butter

½ cup unsweetened canned coconut milk

1 cup chicken stock

Salt, ground black pepper, and cayenne pepper to taste

Nutmeg

Peel and seed the calabaza and cut it into small pieces. In a saucepan, combine the calabaza with water to cover by 2 to 3 inches and bring to a boil. Reduce the heat to medium and simmer, uncovered, until the calabaza begins to soften, about 25 minutes. Remove from the heat and drain, reserving the cooking liquid. Set the squash and liquid aside separately.

Mince the onion and garlic. Peel and chop the tomatoes. In a large saucepan over medium heat, melt the butter. Add the onion and garlic and saute until softened, about 5 minutes. Add the tomatoes and continue to saute for another 2 to 3 minutes. Then add the calabaza, coconut milk, stock, and 2 cups of the reserved cooking liquid and bring to a boil over high heat. Reduce the heat to low, cover, and cook until the squash is very tender when pierced with a fork, about 30 minutes.

Remove from the heat and let cool slightly. Working in batches, puree the soup in a blender or a food processor. Return the pureed soup to the saucepan and place over medium heat. Season with the salt and black and cayenne peppers. Simmer for 10 minutes to blend the flavors.

Ladle into bowls. Grate a dusting of nutmeg over each serving.

Serves 4 to 6

About The Calabaza A cousin of the common American pumpkin, the calabaza, or West Indian pumpkin, has sunny yellow flesh and a pale yellow-green exterior. It usually grows quite large, so it is often sold by the wedge. Trinidad cooks use the pulp for making tea breads and buns, while residents of Martinique and Guadalupe combine it with tomatoes, onions, and spices for a curry. In Jamaica, locals favor the calabaza in a cream soup spiked with chili pepper.

The best pumpkin soup I have ever eaten was made by my friend Josephine Premice, an actress and former Katherine Dunham dancer. A group of us were at Josephine's house one night for drinks after a play and everybody was hungry. She very modestly said she had "a little something in the refrigerator." What she had was pumpkin soup, and as is the case with everything Josephine cooks and serves, it was truly memorable. Here is a simpler Caribbean cousin, a hearty main meal soup that needs only crusty bread or rolls to round out the menu. Like many other soups and stews, it tastes even better reheated the day after it is made.

Caribbean Pumpkin Soup with Beef Short Ribs

3 pounds beef short ribs

1 yellow onion

1 green bell pepper

1 fresh thyme sprig

4 quarts water

1 piece calabaza, about 2 pounds

2 scallions

Salt, ground black pepper, and cayenne pepper to taste

In a large, heavy pot, combine the short ribs, whole onion, whole bell pepper, thyme, and water. Bring to a boil, skim off any scum that forms on the surface, reduce the heat to medium-low, and simmer, uncovered, until the short ribs are tender, 1 to 1 ½ hours.

Meanwhile, peel and seed the calabaza and cut it into large pieces. Chop the scallions, including the tender green tops.

Add the calabaza to the pot and continue to simmer until the calabaza is very tender, 30 to 45 minutes, depending on the size of the pieces.

Scoop out and discard the onion, bell pepper, and thyme sprig. Remove the calabaza pieces and puree them in a blender or a food processor with a little of the liquid from the pot. Return the puree to the soup pot and stir to mix fully with the other ingredients. Season with salt and black and cayenne peppers. Simmer for 10 minutes to blend the flavors, then stir in the scallions. Ladle into bowls and serve piping hot.

Serves 6 to 8

versions of black bean soup appear throughout the Americas. This simple recipe includes onions, garlic, and celery, which are sauteed first to bring out their flavors before adding them to the beans. A little chopped tomato could be cooked along with them. This soup is a favorite of my daughter Chandra.

Chandra's Cuban-style Black Bean Soup

Pick over the black beans, discarding any misshapen beans or grit, and rinse in cold water. Bring a heavy saucepan filled with water to a boil. Add the beans and cook, uncovered, for 5 minutes. Remove from the heat and let cool, then drain. Transfer the beans to a bowl, add water to cover, and refrigerate overnight.

The next day, drain again and return to the saucepan. Add the stock, bay leaf, vinegar, 1 teaspoon salt, and smoked meat to the beans and bring to a boil. Boil rapidly for 2 minutes, then reduce the heat to low, cover, and simmer until the beans are soft enough to be mashed against the side of the pot with the back of a spoon, 1½ to 2 hours.

Meanwhile, chop the celery, onions, and garlic. In a skillet over medium heat, warm the oil. Add the chopped vegetables and saute until the onions are translucent and the celery is soft, 5 to 8 minutes.

When the beans are ready, add the sauteed vegetable mixture and the brown sugar, if using, and stir well. Just before serving, taste and adjust the seasonings, and serve.

Serves 6 to 8

2½ cups (1 pound) dried black beans

6 cups chicken stock

1 bay leaf

1 tablespoon distilled white vinegar

1 teaspoon salt, plus salt to taste

½ pound smoked meat such as a smoked turkey wing or a ham hock

2 celery stalks

3 yellow onions

3 or 4 cloves garlic

3 tablespoons olive oil

Pinch of brown sugar (optional)

Ground black pepper to taste

A Brave Cook My daughter Chandra is a great cook because she is brave in the kitchen. She will try any combination, and she doesn't know what a bare pantry is. That means she can put a meal together from two or three items that no one else could ever imagine trying to cook up in the same pot, and then she serves it to you in a grand presentation. I remember the time she made curried grits, which is definitely not part of her Geechee heritage. I have to admit they were quite good, albeit nontraditional.

Some folks are put off by the appearance of tripe and the "odor" it has. Indeed, tripe may look funny and not smell like a rose when you bring it home from the store, but its distinctive texture and flavor work in this soup.

Philly Pepperpot Soup

1 lemon

3 pounds honeycomb tripe

4 or 5 thick slices bacon or 3 tablespoons vegetable oil

1 green bell pepper

3 celery stalks

1 large yellow onion

2 carrots

5 potatoes

2 teaspoons black peppercorns

1 teaspoon dried thyme

1 teaspoon dried marjoram

2 bay leaves

Salt and red pepper flakes to taste

Squeeze the juice from the lemon and rub the tripe well with the juice, then rinse thoroughly in water. Place in a large pot with water to cover by 2 inches and bring to a boil. Reduce the heat to medium-low, cover partially, and boil gently for about 1 hour. Drain well and, when cool enough to handle, cut into 1-inch squares.

Meanwhile, if using the bacon, cut it into small pieces. Seed and chop the bell pepper. Chop the celery and onion, and peel and chop the carrots and the potatoes. Coarsely crush the peppercorns.

In a soup pot over medium-high heat, fry the bacon until crisp and the fat is rendered, 3 to 5 minutes. Using a slotted spoon, transfer to paper towels to drain. Alternatively, warm the vegetable oil. Add the bell pepper, celery, onion, and carrots and sauté until they begin to soften, about 5 minutes. Add the tripe, peppercorns, thyme, marjoram, bay leaves, salt, red pepper flakes, and water to cover by 2 inches. Bring to a boil, stir well, reduce the heat to low, cover, and simmer for 1 hour.

Add the the potatoes and continue to simmer, covered, until the tripe and the potatoes are tender, about 45 minutes longer. Stir in the reserved bacon, taste and adjust the seasonings. Ladle into bowls and serve.

Serves 8

Valley Forge Rations During the Revolutionary War, when General George Washington's troops were encamped at Valley Forge, it was bitter cold and the soldiers were hungry. The general implored the nameless cook, who was said to be a West Indian, to feed his men if he could. The cook's stocks included only tripe and peppercorns, but he nonetheless rose to the challenge. His peppery broth with chewy tripe not only fed the hungry fighters, but, some believed, also made them victorious. Despite its reputed origin, this legendary soup became known as Philadelphia pepperpot rather than Valley Forge, undoubtedly because it later was a popular street-stand offering in the city of Brotherly Love. The nameless cook was a West Indian, which is why the Caribbean's famed pepperpot soup became wartime rations.

In the past, nearly every Caribbean household counted among its possessions a big, black cast-iron kettle for simmering the pepperpot over the fire. Today, that same distinctive pot is seen in kitchens throughout the islands, but it now includes a built-in electrical unit–the ultimate Caribbean crockpot.

Caribbean Pepperpot Soup

Cut the beef into 2-inch cubes. Cut the chicken into serving pieces. In a large, heavy pot, combine the beef, chicken, and cloves with water to cover by about 2 inches. Bring to a boil, skim off any scum that forms on the surface, reduce the heat to low, cover, and simmer until the meats are tender, about 1 ½ hours.

Meanwhile, seed the bell pepper, then chop the bell pepper, onion and chili pepper. Crush the garlic cloves. Peel and seed the calabaza and cut it into small pieces. Cut the okra into 1-inch-thick rounds. Chop the scallions, including the tender green tops.

Just before the meats are ready, warm the oil in a frying pan over medium heat. Add the bell pepper, onion, and garlic and saute until softened, about 5 minutes. Remove from the heat.

Using a large spoon, skim off the fat from the meat broth and discard. Add the bell pepper mixture, the chili pepper, the calabaza, and the okra to the pot, bring to a boil over high heat, reduce the heat to low, and simmer, uncovered, for 30 minutes. Add the scallions, thyme sprig, and coconut milk and simmer for 15 minutes longer. Season with salt and pepper. Remove and discard the thyme sprig. Ladle into bowls and serve.

Serves 8 to 10

- 1 pound beef stew
- 1 stewing chicken, 4 to 5 pounds
- 1 teaspoon cloves
- 1 green bell pepper
- 1 large yellow onion
- 1 fresh chili pepper
- 3 cloves garlic
- 1 piece calabaza, about 1 pound
- 1 pound okra
- 3 scallions
- 1 tablespoon vegetable oil
- 1 fresh sprig thyme
- ½ cup unsweetened coconut milk
- Salt and ground black pepper to taste

About Pepperpots Pepperpot is easily the most famous soup in the Caribbean, where the recipes vary from country to country, town to town, or even household to household. Yams and salted and fresh meats show up in many pots. According to some cooks, the addition of a salted pig's tail makes it an improper pepperpot, while others say the soup must include okra to deserve the name. Still others claim that authenticity only comes when both meat and fowl are in the soup. I even know one cook who makes a pepperpot without meat, and another who makes it with seafood. Sometimes drop dumplings – called spinners in Jamaica – are added during to the pot. It's obvious that pepperpots offer the opportunity for great riffs in the kitchen.

If you like, omit the cream and add 1 large potato, cooked and mashed, with the stock. If the potato thickens the chowder too much, increase the stock to 3 cups.

Corn & Shrimp Chowder

Thinly slice the scallions, including the tender green tops. Cut the kernels from the ears of corn; you should have about 2 cups. Peel the shrimp. Make a shallow incision along the back of each shrimp and lift out and discard the vein-like tract.

In a saucepan over medium heat, melt the butter. Add the scallions and saute until softened, about 3 minutes. Pour in the stock and stir in the corn. Season with salt and white pepper and simmer, uncovered, for 10 minutes.

Pour in the cream, stir well, and add the shrimp. Reduce the heat to low and simmer gently, uncovered, until the shrimp turn pink and begin to curl, about 5 minutes. Taste and adjust the seasonings. Serve piping hot.

Serves 4 to 6

2 scallions

4 ears of corn

1 pound shrimp

3 tablespoons butter

2 cups chicken or fish stock

Salt and white pepper to taste

½ cup heavy cream

Chowder Family Tree According to Webster's, a "chowder", in the strictest sense, is a seafood soup or stew usually based on milk and sometimes on tomatoes. But the term "chowder" also embraces any soup that resembles a classic seafood chowder, and corn chowders are important members of the extended family. Just about everybody along the Atlantic coast grows and eats corn, and has firm beliefs about how to make the best corn chowder. Some cooks insist on pureeing all the kernels for thickening. Others combine pureed and whole kernels. Still others like to mix colors, stirring together pureed yellow kernels with whole white ones.

If you can get them, use fresh congo peas, a.k.a. gungo or pigeon peas. Dried peas are usually available, however, and work fine, so I have given the instructions for them. For those who like it, leftover ham bone, a pickled pig's tail, or a piece of salted meat is a nice addition but isn't necessary. Caribbean cooks sometimes add yams, potatoes, or dumplings.

Caribbean Congo Pea Soup

2 ½ cups (1 pound) dried congo peas (pigeon peas)

4 quarts water, or as needed

1 large yellow onion

1 green bell pepper

Ham bone or other soup meat

1 tablespoon fresh thyme leaves or ½ teaspoon dried thyme

Salt, ground black pepper, and cayenne pepper to taste

Pick over the peas, discarding any misshapen peas or grit, and rinse in cold water. Place in a large bowl with water to cover generously. Let soak overnight.

Drain the peas and place in a large pot. Chop the onion, and seed and chop the bell pepper. Add them along with the ham bone or other meat to the peas. Pour in enough water to cover by 2 inches and bring to a boil. Reduce the heat to low, cover partially, and simmer until the beans are almost tender, about 1 ½ hours.

Add the thyme, salt, and black and cayenne peppers and simmer, uncovered, for 30 minutes longer to blend the flavors. Taste and adjust the seasonings, then serve.

Serves 6 to 8

This recipe was inspired by one created by Sue Armstrong-Bailey that appeared in the _Super Corn Cookoff Cookbook_. Her recipe was in turn adapted from one that was handed down by Creek Indian Chief Waldo Emerson "Dode" McIntosh, of the Creek Indian Nation West. At first I was surprised when I came across a recipe for a Creek Indian pepperpot, but when you consider that the Arawaks and Carib Indians were simmering "pepperpots" in the Americas for generations, this hearty creation seems like a natural addition. Serve with Albuquerque Blue Corn Bread (page 149).

Creek Indian Pepperpot Soup

Chop the onions and place in a large pot with the beef shank and the 3 quarts water. Bring to a boil, skimming off any scum that forms on the top. Reduce the heat to low, cover, and simmer until the beef shank is tender when pierced with a fork, about 3 hours. Remove from the heat, let cool, cover, and refrigerate overnight. The next day, skim off the fat from the surface of the cooking liquid and discard the fat. Remove the shank from the liquid, and cut the meat from the bone. Dice the meat finely. Set aside.

Peel and dice the potato; you should have about 1 cup. Chop the celery; you should have about ½ cup. Seed and chop the bell peppers. Peel and grate the carrot. Cut the okra into ½-inch-thick rounds. Peel and chop the tomatoes; you should have about 2 cups.

Return the pot of cooking liquid to the stove and bring to a boil. Add the potato, celery, bell peppers, carrot, okra, tomatoes, and corn. Reduce the heat to medium-low, cover, and simmer until all the vegetables are very tender, about 1 hour, adding the salt at the halfway point. Stir in the reserved meat and the chili powder.

In a small bowl, stir together the butter, flour, and ½ cup water to make a thin paste. Slowly add the butter mixture to the soup, being careful to disperse it throughout the pot. Raise the heat to medium and bring to a gentle boil. Cook for 5 minutes, then taste and adjust seasonings. Ladle into bowls and serve.

Serves 6 generously

3 yellow onions

1 beef shank, about 2 pounds

3 quarts plus ½ cup water

1 large baking potato

2 celery stalks

2 green bell peppers

1 carrot

½ pound okra

3 or 4 tomatoes

1 cup corn kernels (fresh or frozen)

1 tablespoon salt

2 tablespoons chili powder

1 tablespoon butter, at room temperature

3 tablespoons all-purpose flour

Rich and creamy, this simple Brazilian soup goes together quickly. Similar soups are found throughout the Atlantic coastal Creole community, where locals call the heart of the palm tree, swamp cabbage.

Brazilian Palm Heart Soup

5 cups chicken stock

3 tablespoons rice flour

1 cup milk

1 can (14 ounces) palm hearts

2 egg yolks

Salt, ground black pepper, and cayenne pepper to taste

Yolks from 2 hard-cooked eggs

Pour the stock into a saucepan and bring to a simmer over medium heat. Meanwhile, in a small bowl, stir together the rice flour and a few tablespoons of the milk to form a smooth paste. While whisking constantly, slowly pour the rice flour paste into the simmering stock. Add the remaining milk and continue to simmer, stirring constantly, until the mixture thickens slightly, 5 to 6 minutes.

Remove from the heat and strain through a fine-mesh sieve into a clean saucepan. Drain the palms hearts and slice crosswise. Add to the pan and bring to just below a boil. Meanwhile, beat the egg yolks in a small bowl. Ladle out about ½ cup of the boiling soup and slowly whisk it into the beaten egg yolks. Then whisk the yolk mixture into the soup. Heat gently, but do not boil.

Season with salt and black and cayenne peppers and ladle into bowls. Crumble the egg yolks with a fork, sprinkle over the tops, and serve.

Serves 4 to 6

Swamp Cabbage Festival The state tree of Florida is the cabbage palm, and although it is protected today, in the past it was regularly harvested and every part was used: the leaves were woven into baskets and mats, the logs were fashioned into pilings, and the heart, known as swamp cabbage, was savored in everything from soups and salads to cakes and cookies. The heart is still prized at the table, as is evidenced by the annual Swamp Cabbage Festival held in La Belle, Florida, in February, where stewed swamp cabbage and crisp, hot swamp cabbage fritters are served up in generous portions.

Salads

Ideally this salad is made with the flesh of three different watermelon varieties: yellow, deep red, pale red, and white are all possible colors. If you cannot find a mix of hues, cantaloupe and/or honeydew can be substituted. This is a good accompaniment to smoked chicken or thinly sliced smoked ham.

Summertime Three-Melon Salad

3 pieces watermelon, each a different variety and each weighing about 1½ pounds

Sugar to taste

Small handful of fresh mint leaves

Fresh orange juice to taste

Pick over and discard any seeds from the watermelons. Using a melon scooper, carve out an equal amount of small balls from each melon variety and place in a large bowl. (Or carve the flesh into small cubes with a sharp knife.) Sprinkle with sugar, mix gently with a large spoon, and cover and chill for several hours, stirring several times.

Just before serving, chop the mint. Sprinkle the orange juice over the salad and garnish with the mint, if desired. Serve chilled.

Serves 8

How To Thump A Watermelon Picking out a ripe watermelon is an art. First, look on its belly – the surface that rested on the ground. If it's very yellow, it's been a long time off the vine and should stay right where it is. If it's green, give it a serious thump with your thumb and index finger. A solid sound means you have a nice, juicy melon. If it rings hollow, pass it up.

Choose Rome Beauty, McIntosh, or a similar apple variety for this salad. The mixture needs the sweet touch of a red apple. Dice everything the same size so the texture is uniform.

Apple & Peanut Salad

3 red apples

1 small green bell pepper

1 carrot

1 celery stalk

Dressing

½ cup mayonnaise

2 tablespoons unsalted smooth peanut butter

1 teaspoon honey

Salt to taste

To make the salad, peel, halve, and core the apples. Seed the bell pepper and peel the carrot. Cut the apples, bell pepper, carrot and celery into the same-sized dice. You should have about 2 cups apples, ¼ cup each celery and bell pepper, and ½ cup carrot. Combine them in a large salad bowl and toss well.

To make the dressing, combine the mayonnaise, peanut butter, and honey in a small bowl and stir until smooth. Season with salt.

Gradually add the dressing to the salad, stirring gently so as not to break up the ingredients. Serve at once. (If you must hold the salad for a while before serving, cover and refrigerate.)

Serves 4

Peanut Butter Origins According to legend, the members of an ancient tribe of South American Indians were the first people to make and eat peanut butter. But most food historians give credit for its invention to an obscure St. Louis physician who came up with the recipe in 1890, as a health food for the elderly. In 1903, Ambrose Straub patented a machine to make the new product, although his design came some eight years after John Harvey Kellogg, the cereal king, filed a patent for a process to prepare "nut meal."

In this old-time companion to barbecued brisket and other hot-weather fare, the beans become trapped inside the pasta shells, producing flavorsome mouthfuls. Elbow macaroni can also be used.

Southern Pasta & Bean Salad

Bring a large pot of water to a boil. Add the pasta and cook until tender but still firm, 10 to 12 minutes or according to the package directions. Drain well in a colander, rinse under cold water, and drain well again. Place in a large bowl.

Drain all the beans and add to the pasta. Chop the red onion and scallions (including the tender green tops) and add them as well. Mix thoroughly, then add the dressing, salt, and pepper and toss gently. Taste and adjust the seasonings, cover, and refrigerate for at least 5 hours, or as long as overnight, to blend the flavors.

Bring to room temperature before serving. Mince the parsley and scatter a little over the top.

Serves 8 to 10

1 pound small pasta shells

1 can (15 ounces) red kidney beans

1 can (15 ounces) garbanzo beans

1 can (15 ounces) Great Northern or other small white beans

1 red onion

3 scallions

About 1 cup favorite Italian dressing

Salt and ground black pepper to taste

Small handful of fresh parsley leaves

Macaroni Salad Throughout the South, macaroni salad is a favorite, traveling to every potluck, church supper, and picnic — in a cooler, of course. Until recently, elbow macaroni was just about the only pasta you ever saw at these functions, but now even the traditional cooks of the Atlantic coastal Creole community are updating their shelves. Today, at these same events you'll see salads made with every pasta shape from farfalle to fusilli.

For a more varied salad, add the same seasonings but use a mix of beans, such as black-eyed peas, red kidneys, Great Northerns, garbanzos, and cut green beans.

Black-eyed Pea Salad

2 ½ cups (1 pound) dried black-eyed peas

½ small yellow bell pepper

½ small green bell pepper

½ small red bell pepper

½ small red onion

1 celery stalk

2 scallions

½ to 1 cup favorite Italian dressing

Salt and ground black pepper to taste

Handful of fresh parsley sprigs

Handful of fresh basil sprigs

Pick over the black-eyed peas, discarding any misshapen peas or grit and rinse in cold water. Place in a large bowl with water to cover generously. Let soak overnight.

The next day, drain the peas and place in a large pan with water to cover by about 2 inches. Bring to a boil, reduce the heat to low, cover partially, and simmer until the peas are tender but still firm, 1 to 1 ½ hours. Drain well and place in a large bowl. Let cool.

Seed and chop all of the bell peppers. Chop the red onion and celery. You should have about ¼ cup of each. Then chop the scallions, including the tender green tops. Add the bell peppers, red onion, celery, and scallions to the peas and mix gently with your hands or a wooden spoon. Add ½ cup of the dressing and stir to mix well. Then slowly add more dressing to taste and season with salt and pepper. Cover and refrigerate overnight, stirring every now and again.

About 2 hours before serving, remove the salad from the refrigerator. Chop the parsley and basil; you should have about ¼ cup of each. Add to the salad. Mix gently and taste and adjust seasonings. Serve at room temperature.

Serves 4 to 6

Putting up Black-eyed Peas As a child I remember watching the women shell mountains of fresh black-eyed peas, and then put them up in big glass jars for eating during the cold months. When my family moved to Philadelphia, I'd return to South Carolina in the summers, and carry some of those jars on the train back to my new home. I was told to keep my eyes on the peas. If the train began to sway on the tracks, I would jump up and grab the jars off the luggage rack and balance them in my lap, to protect against a serious shake-up during the journey north.

The recipe for the original Waldorf salad, which was conceived by chef Oscar Tschirsky of New York's famed Waldorf Astoria Hotel, was first published in 1896. It has been enjoyed throughout the South ever since, with many variations on the original. Here, I have added carrots and raisins and used peanuts in place of the more common walnuts. Pecans are also a possibility.

Peanut Waldorf Salad

½ cup raisins

1½ cups water

3 medium-sized apples

2 celery stalks

1 small carrot

½ cup roasted peanuts

1 lemon

About 2 tablespoons mayonnaise

Place the raisins in a bowl. Bring the water to a boil and pour over the raisins. Let stand until the raisins are plump, about 10 minutes, then drain well and transfer to paper towels to dry.

Peel and core the apples and cut into ½-inch pieces; you should have about 2 cups. Place in a large bowl. Chop the celery and grate the carrot and add to the apples. Coarsely chop the peanuts and add them as well. Squeeze the juice from the lemon into the bowl and toss to mix. (The lemon juice prevents the apples from darkening and adds flavor.) Then gently stir in the mayonnaise until all the ingredients are evenly coated. Serve immediately.

Serves 4

School Days I was ten years old when my family moved to Philadelphia. On one of my first days at school, a classmate offered me some "peanuts," holding up her closed fist. My mother had warned me about the ill-mannered children up North, and because I had never heard the word "peanuts" before, I was afraid my new friend might be enticing me with some forbidden item. But then she uncurled her fingers and there lay a small pile of what I had always known as goobers.

Here, I have used distilled white vinegar, but cooks differ on just what delivers the correct tartness to a coleslaw. Some like a wine vinegar, red or white, while others even tout raspberry vinegar. This coleslaw tastes best if it stays overnight in the refrigerator, so the flavors deepen and blend. Change the recipe as you like: omit the onion, for example, or add raisins, or even peanuts to make a peanut cabbage slaw.

Old-fashioned Coleslaw

Core and finely shred the red and green cabbages. Peel and shred the carrots. Place the cabbages and carrots in a large bowl. Mince the onion and add it to the bowl. Toss to mix well.

Add the vinegar and toss again. Then slowly mix in the mayonnaise, being careful to coat all the ingredients evenly. Transfer to a smaller bowl. Mix in the celery seeds and season with salt and pepper. Cover and chill for at least several hours, but preferably overnight. Serve cold.

Serves 6

½ medium-sized red cabbage

½ medium-sized green cabbage

2 carrots

1 yellow onion

¼ cup distilled white vinegar

About 1 cup mayonnaise

1 teaspoon celery seeds

Salt and ground black pepper to taste

Barbecue And Slaw When people say barbecue, everyone automatically thinks coleslaw. If you are firing up the grill away from home, just pack the slaw in a cooler and carry it along to the beach or park. And don't pass up one of life's great sandwiches: layer slices of barbecued beef brisket (page 98) on a hard roll, top them with coleslaw, throw on some of your favorite barbecue sauce, hold it tight, and bite.

canned beets are a pantry staple and can be served in a variety of ways: julienned and dressed with oil and vinegar; diced, combined with equal amounts of diced carrots and potatoes, and dressed with mayonnaise for a Haitian-style salad; sliced and tossed with a sweet-sour sauce. But for this salad I use fresh beets, and bake rather than boil them for a sweeter result.

Fresh Beet Salad

Preheat an oven to 350 degrees F.

If the beet tops are still attached, cut them off, leaving about ½ inch of the stem intact. (Save the tops for another meal.) Scrub the beets but do not peel. Try not to break their skins or they will "bleed" during cooking. Dry well.

Cut a large sheet of aluminum foil and place the beets in a single layer. Bring up the sides of the foil and seal the edges securely closed. Put the foil package in a baking dish or pan and place in the oven. Bake until tender, 30 to 40 minutes if the beets are small and up to 1 hour if they are large. To test, open a corner of the package and pierce a beet with a sharp knife; if it goes in easily, it is ready. Remove from the oven and unwrap. Let the beets cool, then peel, slice, and put into a bowl.

Make a dressing: In a small bowl, combine 1 part cider vinegar to 3 parts peanut oil (or to your taste). Mix well and season with salt and pepper.

Pour the dressing over the beets and toss well. Cover and chill for several hours to allow the beets to take on the flavor of the dressing. Serve chilled.

Each pound of beets serves 3 or 4

2 to 3 pounds fresh beets

Cider vinegar

Peanut oil

Salt and ground black pepper to taste

Greens Attack In the early 1970's, I was staying in an apartment in Stockholm, Sweden, and I came down with a "greens attack." Swedish food was very good, but my body longed for a plate of greens – turnip, mustard, kale, anything green. In a market I saw a bushel of discarded beet tops. I asked the merchant "how much?" and he kindly gave them all to me. I took them back to my kitchen, cleaned and cut them up, and then cooked them with a little bacon for seasoning. I had a potful. Fixed me some rice and I was prepared to have greens for a week. But the word got out, and every Southerner in Stockholm found their way to my kitchen table.

Since this Brazilian-inspired recipe calls for both canned beets and canned palm hearts, it goes together in just a few minutes, making it ideal for those days when unexpected guests drop in at mealtime.

Palm Hearts & Beet Salad

1 small yellow onion

1 can (8 ounces) sliced beets

1 can (14 ounces) palm hearts

2 tablespoons mayonnaise

Salt and ground black pepper to taste

1 lemon

Bibb lettuce leaves

2 or 3 tomatoes

Small handful of fresh cilantro leaves

Finely chop the onion and place in a bowl. Drain the beets and the palm hearts. Thinly slice the palm hearts and add them and the beets to the onion. Mix in the mayonnaise, being careful not to break up the beets. Season with salt and pepper. Squeeze the juice from the lemon and add to taste.

Line a platter with the lettuce leaves and arrange the salad in a mound in the center. Slice the tomatoes and arrange them around the edge. Mince the cilantro, sprinkle over the tomatoes, and serve.

Serves 6

Black Orpheus I first fell in love with Brazil when I saw the lyrical 1960 film Black Orpheus. It starred a home girl from Pittsburgh, Pennsylvania, Marpessa Dawn, who was living in Paris when she was discovered by director Marcel Camus. The movie and the music made me want to see Brazil. Then I began reading the novels of Brazilian writer Jorge Amado, who celebrates the life and food of his homeland. I soon longed to taste Brazil as well. Finally, in 1983, I did.

In the South, if you make potato salad without hard-boiled eggs, you could become the subject of endless gossip: "You know about her, don't you? She makes potato salad without hard-boiled eggs." This is an American classic. For the best flavor, cook the potatoes in their skins and add the dressing while they are still warm.

Classic White Potato Salad

Fill a saucepan with enough water to cover the eggs by about 1 inch. Bring the water to a boil and, using a slotted spoon, carefully slip the eggs into the water. Reduce the heat to a very gentle simmer and cook for 10 minutes. Transfer the eggs to a bowl of cold water to cool. Once cool, peel and chop.

While the eggs are cooking, scrub the potatoes but do not peel. Place them in a saucepan with water to cover generously and bring to a boil. Cook until tender but not mushy, 15 to 25 minutes, depending on size. Test for doneness with a fork. Meanwhile, chop the celery, and seed and chop the bell pepper. Chop the scallions, including the tender green tops. In a bowl stir together the pickle relish, dry mustard, and mayonnaise.

When the potatoes are ready, drain well. Let cool until they can be handled, then peel and cut into 1½-inch cubes. Put into a large bowl.

While the potatoes are still warm, add the celery, bell pepper, scallions, eggs, and mayonnaise mixture. Mix gently, being careful not to break up the potatoes. Season with salt and pepper as you work. Cover and chill for a least 5 hours or, preferably, overnight.

Serves 6 to 8

5 eggs

3 pounds white- or red-skinned potatoes

2 celery stalks

½ small green bell pepper

6 scallions

3 tablespoons sweet pickle relish

½ teaspoon dry mustard

1 cup mayonnaise

Salt and ground black pepper to taste

Potato Chronicles Food historian Reay Tannahill credits Peruvians with cultivating the potato some five thousand years ago. But commercial potato growing in the united States dates only to the early 1700's, and then only on a small scale. In those days, people tended to think of the potato as animal rather than people food. Records show that by 1763, Connecticut was exporting potatoes, selling them to West Indian plantation owners who wanted to pay as little as possible for food to feed their slaves. Even as late as the opening years of the twentieth century, the potato was still a questionable candidate for the dinner table. According to food writer Waverly Root, Cooking in Old Creole Ways, published in 1904, included only a single potato recipe, and warned the cook to toss out the "poisonous" cooking water.

Be careful not to overcook the sweet potatoes. They must hold their shape once they are peeled and diced. If you can, use a couple of different varieties of sweet potato for this simple salad. Set out a bowl of it with Auntie Kali's Puerto Rican-style Pork Roast (page 91).

Tropical Sweet Potato Salad

Scrub the sweet potatoes but do not peel. Bring a large saucepan of water to a boil. Add the sweet potatoes and boil until just tender when pierced with a fork, about 30 minutes. Drain well, let cool, and peel. Cut into bite-sized pieces and place in a large bowl.

Peel the pineapple and chop the flesh into bite-sized pieces, removing any tough core portions; you should have about 1½ cups. If you are using the apple, core and peel it, then cut into bite-sized pieces; you should have ¼ cup. Add the pineapple and apple to the sweet potatoes along with the raisins and grated coconut. Mix well.

In a small bowl, stir together the ground spices, vanilla, pineapple juice, and coconut milk. Squeeze the juice from the lime and add it as well, mixing thoroughly. Pour the spice mixture over the sweet potato mixture and turn gently to coat all the ingredients. Cover and chill well before serving.

Serves 6 to 8

4 medium-sized sweet potatoes

½ small pineapple

½ apple (optional)

¼ cup raisins

¼ cup grated dried coconut

Pinch of ground cinnamon

Pinch of ground cloves

Pinch of ground nutmeg

1 teaspoon vanilla extract

¼ cup pineapple juice

¼ cup unsweetened canned coconut milk

1 lime

A Little Sweet Potato Lore   North Carolina tops the list of sweet potato producers in the United States. Every year, that single state harvests more than five billion pounds of these tasty members of the morning-glory family. What's clipped from all those vines yields flesh that ranges from light to deep yellow and from moist to dry, and a bumper crop of vitamins, minerals, and fiber.

Being a Geechee girl, I thought I knew everything there was to know about rice, but then I realized I'd only known one kind of rice—long-grain white rice. At first I only ate wild rice at other people's tables. I liked it but I never considered cooking it at home. Then one day I roasted a duck and made a wild rice stuffing. There was still some on my shelf from that experiment, so the next time I was making a rice salad, I decided to cook it up and add it to the bowl. This is the successful result.

White & Wild Rice Salad

½ cup wild rice

4 cups water

   Salt to taste

1 cup long-grain white rice

1 small red bell pepper

1 small green bell pepper

1 small yellow bell pepper

1 celery stalk

3 scallions

2 shallots

Dressing

¼ cup olive oil

2 teaspoons fresh lemon juice

   Salt and ground black pepper to taste

Rinse the wild rice and drain. In a heavy saucepan over high heat, combine the wild rice, 2 cups of the water, and salt. Bring to boil, reduce the heat to low, cover, and cook until tender, 30 to 40 minutes. Remove from the heat, drain off any liquid and let cool.

Meanwhile, in a heavy saucepan over high heat, combine the white rice and the remaining 2 cups water. Bring the water to a boil, cover the pan with a tight-fitting lid, turn down the heat to very low, and cook until the rice is tender and the liquid is absorbed, about 20 minutes. Remove from the heat and let cool.

While the rices are cooking, seed and chop the bell peppers; you should have about ½ cup of each. Chop the celery, scallions (including the tender green tops), and shallots.

To make the dressing, stir together the oil, lemon juice, and salt and pepper in a small bowl, mixing well.

In a large bowl, combine the cooled rices and toss to mix. Add the bell peppers, celery, scallions, and shallots; toss again. Drizzle with the dressing, mixing well to coat the rices evenly, then serve.

Serves 6

About Wild Rice First of all, despite its name, wild rice is not a rice at all, but an aquatic grass that is prized for its long, deep brown grains. The grass grows wild in the fresh and brackish waters of Michigan, Minnesota, and other states east of the Rockies, where harvesting is often done by hand and is regulated to prevent any threat of extinction. Wild rice is cultivated in California, where machines do the work.

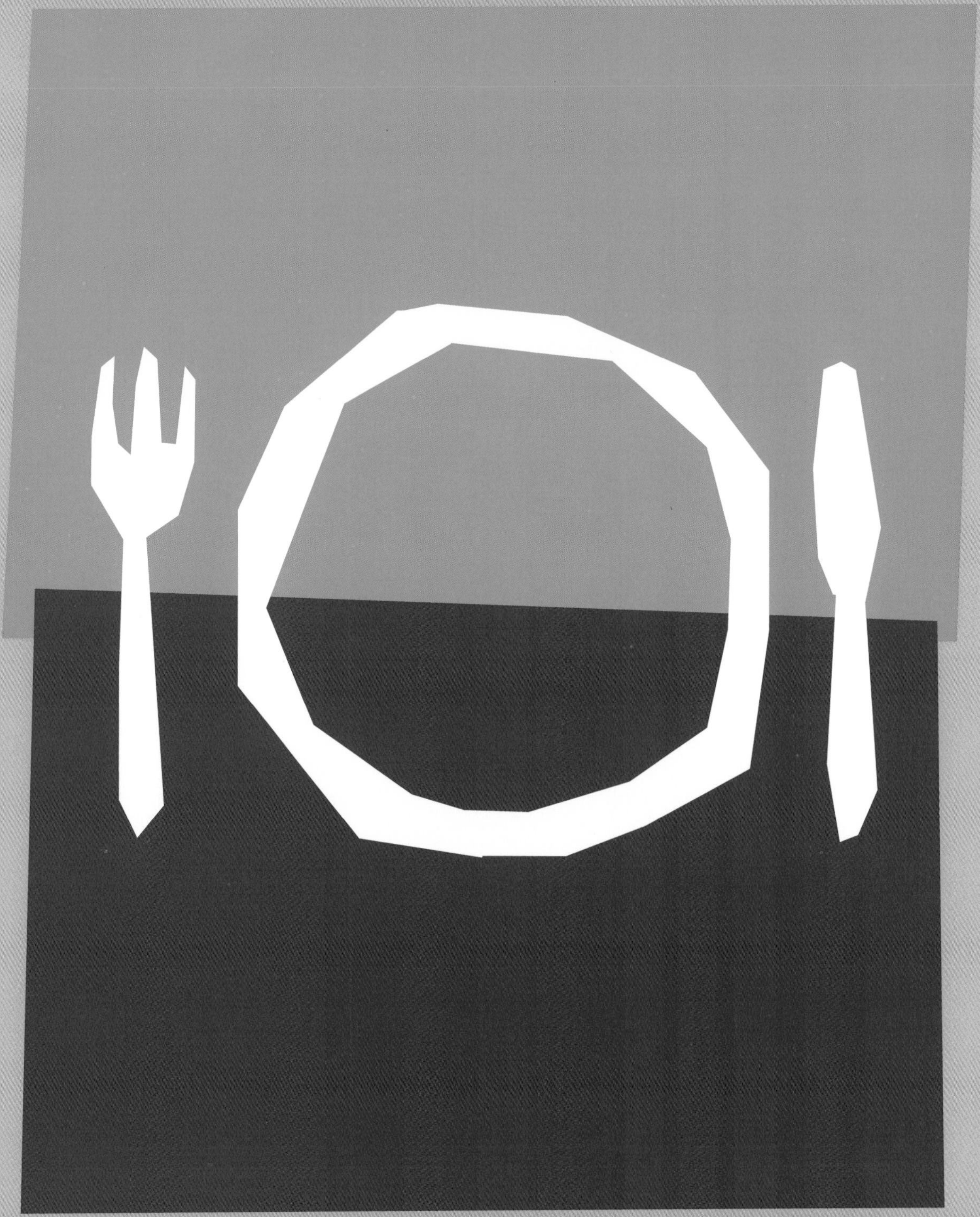

Main Dishes

Try this gingery salsa with meaty fish fillets such as sea bass, monkfish, or grouper.

Broiled Fish with Peanut Salsa

Salsa

- 1 cup roasted peanuts
- 4 or 5 tomatoes
- 1 small yellow onion
- 1 clove garlic

  Fresh ginger
- 1 or 2 fresh jalapeño peppers

  Fresh cilantro leaves

  About ½ cup olive oil

  Salt to taste

- 2 pounds meaty fish fillets

  Olive oil

  Salt and black pepper to taste

First make the salsa: Coarsely chop the peanuts. Peel and chop the tomatoes; you should have 1½ cups. Finely chop the onion and garlic. Peel away some of the skin from a knob of fresh ginger, then finely grate enough ginger to measure 1 tablespoon. Gauge the number of chili peppers you use according to your own taste, then chop finely, discarding the seeds first if you want a milder salsa. Chop enough cilantro to measure 1 tablespoon. Combine all the ingredients in a bowl and add the olive oil. Stir to mix well, then taste and adjust with salt. Set aside for 4 hours to blend the flavors.

To prepare the fish, preheat a broiler (or if the weather is good and you have an outdoor grill, light a charcoal fire). Lightly brush the fish fillets on both sides with olive oil and sprinkle with salt and pepper. Place on a broiler pan and slip into the broiler about 4 inches from the heat. Broil, turning once, until nicely browned and opaque throughout. The timing will depend on the thickness of the fillets; plan about 4 minutes on each side for fillets ¾ to 1 inch thick. (You may prefer your tuna cooked a little less.)

Serve the fish immediately. Pass the salsa at the table.

Serves 6

Batter Express In the days before airconditioning, when food was cooked over an open fire, plantation kitchens would get brutally hot. For that reason, most of them were located in separate buildings behind the master's house. Slaves would cook the meals there and then carry them over to the cool dining room. In the course of a meal there was a lot of back and forth and, over time, the pathways taken by these slaves came to be known as the batter express.

Mullet has bones. That means some of you won't like this stew. And when I make it, I use the heads. They give it flavor. To tell the truth, Grandmama Sula used to make a fish stew using just the heads. The very best mullet to use weighs no more than half a pound. The smaller ones are sweeter. The stew is also good over True Grits (page 138).

Mullet Stew

1 yellow onion

1 tomato

1 mullet, 1½ to 2 pounds, cleaned or smaller ones, if available

Salt, ground black pepper, and cayenne pepper to taste

All-purpose flour

¼ cup vegetable oil

½ cup fish stock

Proper Geechee Rice (page 134)

Chop the onion, and peel and chop the tomato.

Rinse the mullet and pat dry with paper towels. Cut the mullet into quarters and then season the fish pieces with salt and black and cayenne peppers. Place the flour in a brown paper bag, add the fish pieces two at a time, and shake the bag to coat the pieces evenly.

In a large skillet over high heat, warm the oil. Add the fish pieces and fry, turning once, until golden on both sides, about 5 minutes on each side. Transfer the fish pieces to a plate.

Remove all but 1 tablespoon of the oil from the skillet and warm over medium heat. Add the onion and saute until softened, about 5 minutes. Return the fish pieces to the skillet and add the tomatoes and stock. Cover and simmer over low heat until the fish flakes easily, about 10 minutes. Taste and adjust the seasonings.

Transfer the fish and the pan sauce to a serving bowl. Pass the rice at the table.

Serves 4

use a liberal hand with the cayenne pepper, because this South Carolina dish with a Bahamian accent should carry some fire. It is delicious served over Caribbean Fungi (page 128) or True Grits (page 138), both of which will help cool the flames.

Low Country Boiled Fish

Rinse the cod steaks and pat dry with paper towels. Sprinkle with salt. Thinly slice the onion. Squeeze the juice from the lemons. Scatter half of the onion slices evenly over the bottom of a glass or ceramic dish. Top with the cod steaks and then the remaining onions. Drizzle the lemon juice evenly over the top. Cover and refrigerate for several hours, turning the fish two or three times while it is marinating.

Remove the cod steaks from the marinade and pat dry with paper towels; reserve the marinade. In a large skillet over medium heat, melt the butter. Add the cod steaks and sauté, turning once, until nicely browned on both sides, about 5 minutes on each side.

Add the reserved marinade and onions and the water and bring to a boil. Cook, uncovered, at a gentle boil for 10 minutes. Season with salt and the black and cayenne peppers and continue to cook, uncovered, until the fish is very tender and steaks have broken up into pieces, about 5 minutes longer. The dish should look like a stew at this point.

Transfer to a serving dish and serve hot.

Serves 3

3 cod steaks, about 6 ounces each

Salt to taste

1 large yellow onion

2 lemons

2 tablespoons butter

1½ cups water

Ground black pepper and cayenne pepper to taste

My Father The Fisherman My father, Frank Smart, loved fishing. As we say in Carolina, he stayed in the creek. His reputation as a terrific fisherman lasted until the day he died. I once asked him how he always won the bet that he could catch the most fish. He replied, "Simple. What I don't catch I buy from other fishermen."

I first ate this fish dish in the Bahamas, where a grouper was used instead of bass. There, the wrapped fish was cooked on a charcoal grill. At home I make it in the oven.

Baked Bass with Vegetables

1 yellow onion

1 small zucchini

1 small yellow summer squash

1 large carrot

2 new potatoes, about 5 ounces each

1 large tomato

3 tablespoons butter

1 whole striped bass, cleaned, 4 to 5 pounds

Salt and ground black pepper to taste

2 or 3 fresh parsley sprigs

2 or 3 fresh thyme sprigs

2 lemons

¼ cup dry white wine

Chop the onion. Trim the zucchini and yellow squashes and cut into slices ½ inch thick. Peel the carrot and cut into slices ½ inch thick. Scrub the potatoes but do not peel; cut into slices ½ inch thick. Cut the tomato into 8 wedges.

Bring a saucepan filled with water to a boil and add the carrot slices. Parboil for 8 to 10 minutes, then lift out with a slotted spoon and set aside. Add the potato slices to the same boiling water and parboil for 8 to 10 minutes, then drain and set aside.

Preheat an oven to 350 degrees F.

Select a baking dish or pan that will accommodate the fish and line it with a piece of heavy-duty aluminum foil that is large enough to enclose the fish completely. (If you do not have a dish or pan that can accommodate the fish, cut off its head or its head and tail.) Rub half of the butter over the foil.

Rinse the fish and pat dry with paper towels. Make 3 diagonal slashes on each side of the fish, then season it inside and out with salt and pepper.

Tuck the parsley and thyme sprigs inside the cavity and place the fish in the dish atop the foil. Scatter the onion, squashes, carrot, potatoes, and tomato wedges over and around the fish.

(continued on page 68)

Baked Bass with Vegetables (continued)

Squeeze the juice from the lemons and pour it and the wine over the fish and vegetables.

Melt the remaining 1½ tablespoons butter and drizzle over the fish. Bring the edges of the foil together and seal them securely.

Place in the oven and bake until the fish is cooked, about 25 minutes. To test, open the foil wrapper at a point where you can insert a knife blade into the thickest part of the fish; the flesh should flake easily. Be careful not to overcook.

Using two large spatulas, one at either end of the fish, transfer the bass to a large platter. Spoon the vegetables and pan juices over and around the fish. Serve immediately.

Serves 6

Fresh Fish How can you tell if a fish is fresh? The first thing to do is to look into its eyes. They should be bright and free of any cloudiness. Press a fingertip against its belly. The flesh should bounce right back. The gills should be brilliant red. And finally, sniff your potential purchase. It should smell like a fish, but not smell fishy.

catfish are so named because the feelers that extend from each side of their heads resemble feline whiskers. In times past, the taste of catfish was risky and these earthy river denizens were much maligned. Mark Twain was a believer, however, insisting "catfish is a plenty good enough fish for anybody." Today, of course, they are farm bred and very popular. A side of hush puppies is a must.

Fried Catfish

Rinse the catfish fillets and pat dry with paper towels. Season generously on both sides with salt and pepper. Place the cornmeal in a brown paper bag, add the fillets a couple at a time, and shake the bag to coat the fillets evenly.

Pour the oil into a large, heavy skillet (preferably cast iron) to a depth of about 1½ inches. Heat until hot but not smoking. When the oil is ready, slip the catfish into the skillet, adding only as many fillets as will fit without crowding. If there is too much fish in the pan at once, the oil temperature will drop and the fish will absorb too much oil. Fry until golden brown on the first side, 3 to 5 minutes. Flip the catfish over and continue to fry until golden brown on the second side, 3 to 5 minutes longer. The timing will depend upon the thickness of the fillets. Using a slotted spatula, lift out the fillets and place on paper towels to drain.

Serve the catfish fillets piping hot with the Hush Puppies on the side.

Serves 4

4 catfish fillets, 5 to 6 ounces each

Salt and ground black pepper to taste

Yellow or white cornmeal

Vegetable oil for frying

Hush Puppies (page 142)

Black Watermen There is a long tradition of black watermen in the South. Remember the Mosquito Fleet in Gershwin's Porgy and Bess? It was based on real fishermen who took their name from the fact that their boats were often so far out in the water that from the shore they looked like mosquitos. In Charleston, many of the watermen lived in a district known as Cabbage Row because of the vegetable vendors who resided there. In Gershwin's play that neighborhood became Catfish Row. I am told that there are still a couple of seniors around who remember the real-life Porgy. Small, freshly caught whole fish – croakers, mullets, spots, butterfish, whiting, and especially porgies – are fried up by cooks all along the Atlantic coast of the legendary black watermen.

This is the national dish of Jamaica, a traditional breakfast plate that symbolizes the morning meal in the same way that ham and eggs do stateside. In fact, although ackee is a tropical fruit, it looks like scrambled eggs. Outside of the Caribbean and Africa, ackee is rarely found fresh, but you can find it canned in specialty-food stores and the international section of some well-stocked supermarkets.

Ackee & Saltfish

1 pound boneless saltfish

2 tomatoes

3 scallions

1 small yellow onion

1 small green bell pepper

1 can (14 ounces) ackee

2 thick slices bacon

Chopped fresh chili pepper to taste

¼ cup coconut oil or vegetable oil

Salt and ground black pepper to taste

Place the saltfish in a good-sized bowl and add cold water to cover. Refrigerate for about 12 hours, changing the water every few hours. Drain and remove and discard any skin and errant bones. (You may need to soak the fish longer, depending on its hardness, thickness, and saltiness; it should feel somewhat supple.) Using your fingers, flake the fish and set aside. (At this point, some cooks boil the saltfish for 10 to 20 minutes before flaking, but I don't.)

Peel and chop the tomatoes. Chop the scallions (including the tender green tops), yellow onion, and bell pepper. Drain the ackee.

Cut the bacon into small pieces. In a large skillet over medium-high heat, fry the bacon until crisp, 3 to 5 minutes. Using a slotted spoon, transfer to paper towels to drain. Pour off the excess fat from the skillet.

Add the oil to the same skillet and place over medium heat. Add the tomato, scallions, yellow onion, bell pepper, and chili pepper and saute until softened, about 5 minutes. Add the bacon, saltfish, and ackee and season with salt and black pepper. Stir well, cover, and simmer over low heat until the fish is tender and the flavors have blended, 5 to 10 minutes. Serve hot.

Serves 4 to 6

The Smiling Fruit Ackee is native to West Africa and was brought to Jamaica in the eighteenth century by the legendary Captain William Bligh. The red, pear-shaped fruit is poisonous and rather solemn looking until fully ripened, at which point it is no longer toxic and "bursts into a smile" to reveal three shiny black seeds and yellow flesh the color of scrambled eggs. There is even a riddle about the dangers of picking an ackee before it's ready: "My father sent me to pick out a wife and told me to take only those with a smile. Those without a smile, he said, will kill me. What is my wife?" The answer, of course, is ackee.

In Jamaica, these tasty fritters are called stamp and go. Some claim the name comes from an old sailing term meaning "hurry up." Another common explanation is that it describes how the fritters are made: "stamped" out between the palms, fried briefly, and then eaten on the "go."

Main Dishes 71

Saltfish Fritters

Place the saltfish in a good-sized bowl and add cold water to cover. Refrigerate for about 12 hours, changing the water every few hours. Drain and place in a saucepan. Add water to cover and bring to a boil. Reduce the heat to medium and simmer, uncovered, until the fish is tender and flakes easily, 10 to 20 minutes. (The cooking time will depend on the hardness and thickness of the fish and how fully it has been reconstituted in the soaking.) Drain well and let cool. Remove and discard any skin and errant bones. Using your fingers, flake the fish into a bowl.

Mince the onion, then seed and mince the chili. Add them to fish. In another bowl, mix together the flour and baking powder. Lightly beat the egg and stir it into the dry ingredients along with ¾ cup water or stock. Stir until a thick, smooth batter forms with the consistency of mashed potatoes. If the batter is too stiff, add more liquid. But be careful: you don't want it to be like pancake batter.

Pour the oil into a heavy skillet to a depth of ½ inch. Place over medium-high heat and heat until the oil is hot but not smoking. Working in batches, carefully drop the batter into the hot oil, using a heaping tablespoonful to form each fritter. Do not crowd the skillet. Fry, turning once, until golden brown on both sides, about 5 minutes total. Using a slotted utensil, transfer to paper towels to drain. These fritters are best served hot, right out of the skillet.

Makes about 2 dozen fritters; serves 4

½ pound boneless saltfish

1 yellow onion

1 small fresh chili pepper

1 cup flour

1 teaspoon baking powder

1 egg

¾ cup water or stock, or as needed

Vegetable oil for frying

About Saltfish A mainstay of the Caribbean, saltfish is variously known as Bacalhau (Portuguese), baccala (Italian), bacalao (Spanish), and as salt cod or dried cod in the United States. The salting and drying of foods was introduced to the Caribbean by the Africans and the Europeans. In the absence of refrigeration, this new method was quickly adopted as a good means of preserving not only fish, but also a variety of meats.

Daufuskie cooks hold on to their recipes like misers hold on to their money, so this recipe is from my taste memory of Daufuskie's outstanding culinary accomplishment, deviled crab. On the island, they pack the mixture into crab backs, but little ramekins will do.

Daufuskie Island Deviled Crab

Prepare an oven to 350 degrees F.

Seed and chop the bell pepper, and chop the onion. Crush enough biscuits to measure 2 tablespoons.

In a bowl, combine the crab meat, bell pepper, onion, biscuit crumbs, mustard, and 2 tablespoons mayonnaise. Season with the salt, lots of black pepper, and the cayenne pepper. Stir to mix. Squeeze 1 tablespoon juice from the lemon and add to the bowl. Stir again. If the mixture isn't holding together, add more mayonnaise.

Grease 8 crab backs or an equal number of small ramekins with the butter. Divide crab mixture evenly among them. Bake until heated through and lightly browned, 20 to 30 minutes. Serve hot.

Serves 8

½ small green bell pepper

1 yellow onion

A few Needa biscuits or plain crackers

1 pound lump crab meat

1 teaspoon dry mustard

2 tablespoons mayonnaise, or as needed

Salt, ground black pepper, and cayenne pepper to taste

1 lemon

2 tablespoons butter

Daufuskie Island The only island in South Carolina without a bridge connecting it to the mainland, Daufuskie is close to Savannah and for generations residents took their produce down the intercoastal roadway to market there. Following Emancipation, the blacks stayed on the island and farmed and fished, and little attention was paid to Daufuskie or the other Sea Islands by the mainlanders. For several decades, an oyster plant provided employment, and Daufuskie oysters were said to be among the finest in the world, reportedly even enjoyed by the Russian tsars. The 1974 film Conrack, based on Pat Conroy's The Water Is Wide about teaching in the Daufuskie school, brought some recognition to the island, but by 1980 there were fewer than 100 permanent residents. Today, golf courses and weekend homes have been built by mainlanders, and residents who can trace their roots back to the Emancipation number fewer than 40.

To many people, the combination of shellfish, chilies, and nuts means Asian dishes. But the Atlantic coastal Creole community has long enjoyed this happy marriage of flavors.

Shrimp & Goobers

1   pound large shrimp

Salt and ground black pepper to taste

Fresh ginger

2   cloves garlic

4   scallions

1   or more fresh green chili peppers

⅓   cup roasted peanuts

2   tablespoons vegetable oil

Small handful of fresh cilantro leaves

Peel the shrimp. Make a shallow incision along the back of each shrimp and lift out and discard the vein-like tract. Sprinkle with salt and black pepper and refrigerate until needed.

Peel away some of the skin from a knob of fresh ginger, then finely grate enough ginger to measure 1 teaspoon. Mince the garlic cloves. Chop the scallions, including the tender green tops. Gauge the number of chilies you use according to your own taste, then chop finely, discarding the seeds first if you want a milder dish. Finely chop the peanuts. Set all the ingredients near the stove.

In a large, heavy skillet over medium heat, warm the vegetable oil. Add the ginger and garlic and cook for a minute or two to release their fragrance. Add the shrimp and stir until they are coated with the oil. Stir in the scallions and chilies and cook for 1 minute. Add the peanuts and salt and cook, stirring often, until the shrimp turn pink and curl, about 2 minutes longer.

Meanwhile, mince the cilantro. Transfer the shrimp mixture to a platter and sprinkle with the cilantro. Serve hot.

Serves 4

Shrimp Count Shrimp are graded according to size - small, medium, large, extra large, jumbo - and each size measures out at a certain number of shellfish per pound. For example, there are usually 21 to 30 large shrimp per pound, and 16 to 20 extra large. Despite these standards, some fishmongers will try to sell you "large" shrimp that are no bigger than what we use for bait in South Carolina. The best solution is to find a trustworthy fishmonger and return often. Also, be sure to check out rock shrimp, which are native to the Atlantic from Virginia south into the waters around the Bahamas. They are a little more difficult to peel because of their hard shells, but they have a wonderful sweet, lobster-like taste.

This is a Brazilian *moqueca*, a stew made with any fish or shellfish or a mixture of the two. The dendê oil gives the dish a beautiful yellow-orange cast and a distinctive taste and aroma. Bahians say "the smell opens the appetite." Look for the oil in Latin American markets. You can, if you like, use peanut oil, but the flavor of the dish will be "off." Serve over rice.

Bahian Shrimp Stew

Peel the shrimp. Make a shallow incision along the back of each shrimp and lift out and discard the vein-like tract. Peel and chop the tomato. Seed and chop the bell pepper. Chop the onion, and garlic.

In a skillet over medium heat, warm the olive oil. Add the tomato, onion, bell pepper, and garlic and sauté until softened, about 5 minutes. Add the coconut milk and tomato paste, stir well, and simmer, uncovered, for 5 minutes.

Meanwhile, chop enough cilantro to measure 1 tablespoon and squeeze the juice from the lemon(s).

Add the shrimp and the *dendê* oil to the skillet and simmer until the shrimp turn pink and curl, 5 to 8 minutes longer. When the shrimp are ready, season the stew to taste with lemon juice, salt, and black pepper and stir in the cilantro. Serve hot.

Serves 4

1 pound large shrimp

1 large tomato

1 small green bell pepper

1 large yellow onion

2 cloves garlic

3 tablespoons olive oil

⅔ cup unsweetened canned coconut milk

2 tablespoons tomato paste

2 fresh cilantro leaves

1 or 2 lemons

2 tablespoons *dendê* oil (see page 24)

Salt and ground black pepper to taste

The Bahian Kitchen Located on the northern coast of Brazil, the city of Bahia is famous throughout South America for its extraordinary cuisine rich in African influences. The Bahian cooks of today owe much to the slaves brought to the surrounding area in the sixteenth century by the Portuguese, who put them to work in the sugarcane fields. Arguably the slaves' most important contribution to the Bahian pantry was dendê oil, a distinctive orange-red cooking oil extracted from the fruit of a West African palm that now thrives in Brazil.

Perlou, pirlou, perloo, perlew. They all mean the same thing. This is the signature rice dish of South Carolina. It can be made with shrimp, as it is here, or with meats, sausage, vegetables-really, anything you have in the pantry.

South Carolina Shrimp Perlou

Peel the shrimp, reserving the shells. Make a shallow incision along the back of each shrimp and lift out and discard the vein-like tract. Cover and refrigerate the shrimp.

Place the shrimp shells in a saucepan and add the water and the crab boil seasoning. Bring to a boil, reduce the heat to medium-low, and simmer, uncovered, for 15 minutes. Remove from the heat and strain the stock through a fine-mesh sieve into a measuring pitcher; you should have 2 cups. Set the stock aside.

Meanwhile, chop the onion and mince the garlic. Peel and chop the tomatoes. In a heavy skillet over medium-high heat, cook the bacon until crisp, 3 to 5 minutes. Using a slotted spoon, remove to paper towels to drain. Add the onion, garlic, and rice to the bacon drippings remaining in the skillet and cook, stirring frequently, until all the ingredients are coated with the oil and the rice kernels are beginning to turn opaque, 3 to 4 minutes.

Add the tomatoes, salt, pepper, and the reserved 2 cups stock. Bring to a boil over medium-high heat, reduce the heat to low, cover, and cook until the liquid is nearly absorbed, 20 to 30 minutes.

Stir in the shrimp, re-cover, and cook until the shrimp turn pink and the liquid is fully absorbed, 5 to 8 minutes. Transfer to a serving dish, crumble the bacon over the top, and serve.

Serves 6

1 pound medium-sized shrimp

2 ½ cups water

2 tablespoons favorite crab boil

1 small yellow onion

3 cloves garlic

2 tomatoes

3 thick slices bacon

1 cup long-grain white rice

Salt and ground black pepper to taste

Here, the shells from the shrimp are used to make a stock, to give the finished dish a fuller shellfish flavor. Many cooks simmer the shrimp too long in this famed Creole dish. I add them near the end and cook them rather briefly, knowing that the stock will have already imparted the needed shrimp flavor. You can also allow the dish to cool, refrigerate it overnight, and then reheat just to serving temperature the next day. The overall bouquet of the stew will deepen during its nighttime rest.

Shrimp Creole

2	pounds medium-sized shrimp
2	yellow onions, 1 small and 1 medium
4	celery stalks
4	cloves garlic
	Ground black pepper to taste
4	fresh parsley sprigs
1	small green bell pepper
5	tomatoes
¼	cup vegetable oil
	Salt to taste
½	teaspoon cayenne pepper
1	bay leaf

Peel the shrimp, reserving the shells. Make a shallow incision along the back of each shrimp and lift out and discard the vein-like tract. Cover and refrigerate the shrimp.

Make the shrimp stock: Place the shrimp shells in a saucepan and add water to cover. Cut the small onion into quarters. Cut 2 celery stalks in half, and smash 2 garlic cloves. Add them all to the saucepan along with the black pepper and parsley sprigs.

Bring to a boil, reduce the heat to medium-low, and simmer, uncovered, for 15 minutes.

Remove from the heat and strain through a fine-mesh sieve into a measuring pitcher. Pour off 1 cup to use for this recipe.

Cover and store the remainder for another use; it will keep for a few days in the refrigerator or for up to 1 month in the freezer.

Chop the medium onion and the remaining 2 celery stalks and 2 garlic cloves. Seed and chop the bell pepper. Peel and chop the tomatoes.

In a heavy saucepan over medium heat, warm the vegetable oil. Add the celery, onion, and bell pepper and sauté, stirring frequently, until the vegetables are softened, about 5 minutes. Add the 1 cup shrimp stock, the tomatoes, salt, cayenne pepper, and bay leaf.

Bring to a boil, reduce the heat to low, and cook, uncovered, until slightly thickened and the flavors are blended, 25 to 30 minutes.

Stir in the shrimp and cook until the shrimp curl and turn pink, 5 to 8 minutes. Remove and discard the bay leaf. Taste and adjust the seasonings. Transfer to a bowl and serve.

Serves 6

Creole Cooking Creole cooking exists throughout the United States but, in the strictest sense, Creole cooking is the cuisine that developed in southern Louisiana in the early 1700's, when the first French colonists found themselves away from their homeland pantry. Forced to adapt, they combined native ingredients with French cooking methods. In the years that followed, Spanish, African, and West Indian cooks all added new ideas and new ingredients to the Creole kitchen. Today, of course, Southern Creole cooking has spread beyond those early borders.

I know that in Louisiana, "first you roux"—flour and fat slowly browned until the mixture has a nut-like flavor—for their gumbos, but I never use one. There are two camps on how to thicken a gumbo. One camp maintains that filé powder, made from the dried leaves of the sassafras tree, is the only proper thickener. The other believes that okra is the only way to go. I'm with the okra people.

Shrimp & Sausage Gumbo

2 pounds large shrimp

2 cups water

½ pound smoked sausage

1 small yellow onion

2 celery stalks

1 green bell pepper

3 cloves garlic

1 pound okra

1 can (28 ounces) tomatoes

1 tablespoon butter

1 tablespoon olive oil

½ teaspoon salt

½ teaspoon ground black pepper

½ teaspoon dried thyme

1 bay leaf

Cayenne pepper to taste

Proper Geechee Rice (page 134)

4 scallions

Handful of fresh parsley sprigs

Peel the shrimp, reserving the shells. Make a shallow incision along the back of each shrimp and lift out and discard the vein-like tract. Cover and refrigerate the shrimp.

Place the shrimp shells in a saucepan and add the water. Bring to a boil, reduce the heat to medium-low, and simmer, uncovered, for 10 minutes. Remove from the heat and strain the stock through a fine-mesh sieve. Set the stock aside.

Cut the sausage into ¼-inch-thick slices. Chop the onion and celery, and seed and chop the bell pepper. Mince the garlic. Cut the okra into ¼-inch-thick rounds. Open the can of tomatoes and drain them. Chop the tomatoes.

In a large skillet over medium heat, melt the butter with the olive oil. Add the sausage and fry until nicely browned on both sides, about 5 minutes. Using a slotted spoon, remove to a plate and set aside.

Add the onion, celery, bell pepper, and garlic to the skillet and saute until softened, 5 to 8 minutes. Stir in the okra and the tomatoes and mix well. Pour in the shrimp stock and add the salt, black pepper, thyme, bay leaf, and cayenne to taste. Raise the heat to high. Bring to a boil, reduce the heat to low, cover, and cook until the vegetables are soft, the mixture is thickened, and the flavors are blended, about 1 hour.

(continued on page 82)

Shrimp & Sausage Gumbo (continued)

About 30 minutes before the gumbo is ready, cook the rice. Chop the scallions, including the tender green tops. Cut off and discard any tough parsley stems and chop the parsley.

Add the shrimp to the vegetables, stir well, re-cover, and cook until the shrimp turn pink and curl, about 8 minutes. Return the sausage to the pan and heat through. Remove and discard the bay leaf. Taste and adjust the seasonings with salt, black pepper, and cayenne pepper.

To serve, place the rice in individual shallow soup plates and spoon the gumbo over and around it. Sprinkle with the scallions and parsley.

Serves 6

About Gumbo The word "gumbo" arrived in the South with the African slaves. It was their name for okra, a vegetable that had been prized in the Old World since prehistoric times. Over the years, the term evolved to where it more commonly was used for a stew made with the vegetable. But in certain Southern pockets, gumbo remains the name for both the tapered green pods and the stew. So when folks tell you they are making an okra gumbo, they are caught up in a culinary redundancy.

The list of ingredients for this West African dish is as long as a kielbasa sausage. All kinds of meats (fresh and salted), seafood (fresh, smoked, and dried), poultry, and just about every vegetable can go into this hearty one-pot meal.

Jollof Rice

Rinse the chicken and pat dry with paper towels. Cut into serving pieces. Cut the beefsteak into large bite-sized pieces. Seed and chop the bell pepper, and chop the onions, scallions, and garlic. Peel and chop the carrots and tomatoes.

In a large, heavy pot over medium heat, warm the peanut oil. Add the chicken pieces and brown on all sides, 5 to 10 minutes. Using a slotted utensil, transfer the chicken to a plate. Add the beef to the pot and brown it on all sides. Remove to the plate with the chicken. Add the bell pepper, onions, scallions, garlic, carrots, and tomatoes to the same pot and saute over medium heat until they begin to soften, about 10 minutes. Return the chicken and beef to the pot and add the allspice, thyme, salt, black and cayenne peppers, and 3 cups of the stock, or as needed to cover. Bring to a boil, cover, reduce the heat to low, and cook for 45 minutes.

Meanwhile, cut the cabbage into 8 wedges and place on a steamer rack over boiling water. Cover and steam until almost tender, about 10 minutes. Remove from the steamer and set aside.

When the meats have cooked for 45 minutes, stir in the rice. Combine the tomato paste with the remaining stock and add to the pot. Stir well, raise the heat to high, bring to a boil, cover, reduce the heat to low, and cook until the rice is tender, about 20 minutes. Gently stir the cabbage into the rice mixture and cook for 10 minutes longer. Taste and adjust the seasonings, then serve.

Serves 6 to 8

About Jollof Rice This famous dish of West Africa is most often said to have originated with the Wolof people of Gambia. Some food historians, however, say it is from Senegal. If you've read both, don't get steamed. Borders are pretty fluid in those parts. Like its African-American descendant, Low Country red rice (page 135), the only sure thing about jollof rice is that it be red. So don't leave out the tomato paste.

1 chicken, about 3 pounds

2 pounds beefsteak

1 small green bell pepper

2 yellow onions

4 scallions

2 cloves garlic

2 carrots

3 large tomatoes

¼ cup peanut oil

½ teaspoon ground allspice

½ teaspoon dried thyme

Salt, ground black pepper, and cayenne pepper to taste

5 cups chicken or beef stock

½ small green cabbage

2 cups long-grain white rice

1 can (6 ounces) tomato paste

If you are not up to making the Jamaican jerk rub, check out specialty stores and supermarkets. A number of good jerk rubs are currently on the shelves. The rub can also be used for meats and fish. The lantern-shaped Scotch bonnet peppers (also known as habañeros) are fiery mouthfuls popular in the Caribbean; if you can't find them, jalapeños or other hot chilies will do. I have slipped the chicken into an oven, but if you have an outdoor grill, the bird is delicious—and traditionally—cooked over a charcoal fire.

Jerk Chicken

1   yellow onion

8   scallions

¼   cup ground allspice

1   tablespoon ground cinnamon

1   tablespoon ground nutmeg

1   or more Scotch bonnet chili peppers

2   teaspoons salt

Ground black pepper to taste

¼   to ½ cup dark Jamaican rum

1   chicken, about 3 pounds

Cut the yellow onion into chunks and the scallions into 1- or 2-inch lengths. Place them in a blender with the allspice, cinnamon, nutmeg, chili peppers, salt, black pepper, and a few tablespoons of the rum. Process to form a paste. If the mixture is too thick, add more rum and process again. You will have about 1 cup, which is enough for several chickens. The leftover rub can be tightly covered in the refrigerator for up to 2 weeks.

Split the chicken in half, rinse, and pat dry with paper towels. Cover the chicken with the rub; you will need 3 to 4 tablespoons. Place in a non-reactive dish. Cover and refrigerate for several hours.

Preheat an oven to 400 degrees F. Remove the chicken halves from the marinade and place, skin side up, in a baking pan in which they will fit side by side. Cook for 15 minutes. Reduce the heat to 350 degrees F and continue to cook, basting often with the pan juices, until the chicken is tender and the juices run clear when pierced at the thigh, about 30 minutes longer. Transfer the chicken to a platter and serve.

Serves 4

About Jerk In Ochos Rios, Jamaica, I discovered that Jamaicans have seasoned the history of barbecue with a distinctive style and method all their own. They call it jerk, and it is an elaborate process that has been passed down from the maroons, slaves who escaped from their masters in the nineteenth century. The maroons seasoned meat with a complex blend of spices and grilled it over a pimento wood fire. The original purpose of the jerk spice mixture was to preserve the meats in the absence of refrigeration. Today, people jerk more than meat. In Jamaica, I ate jerked fish and breadfruit.

Traditionally this dish is seasoned with salt pork, but I have left it out in this version and it is still very flavorful. I call for cutting a whole chicken into serving pieces, but if you like chicken legs and thighs, they would be good, too. I would not use boneless chicken pieces, as the bone helps to keep the meat succulent. Don't skimp on the saffron. It is expensive, but the flavor, subtle though it is, is worth the money.

Arroz con Pollo

Cut the chicken into serving pieces, rinse, and pat dry with paper towels. Seed the bell pepper, then finely chop the bell pepper, onion, and garlic. Peel and finely chop the tomato. Crumble the saffron threads into ½ cup of the stock.

In a Dutch oven over medium heat, warm the olive oil. Working in batches if necessary, brown the chicken pieces well on all sides, about 10 minutes. Using tongs, remove from the pot and set aside.

Add the onion, bell pepper, and garlic to the same pot and saute over medium heat until softened, about 5 minutes. Stir in the tomatoes, mixing well, then add the rice, coating it well with the oil. Pour in the chicken stock and the saffron and its soaking water and add the bay leaf, salt, black pepper, and red pepper flakes. Raise the heat and bring to a boil. Cover, reduce the heat to low, and cook until the rice is tender and the chicken pieces are cooked through, about 20 minutes.

Uncover the pot, sprinkle the peas evenly over the top, and re-cover. Continue to cook over low heat until the peas are tender, about 5 minutes. Remove from the heat and let rest for 10 minutes. Arrange the chicken and rice on a large platter, discarding the bay leaf. Cut the pimiento into shreds and scatter over the top. Serve hot.

Serves 6 to 8

1 chicken, about 3 pounds

1 green bell pepper

1 yellow onion

3 cloves garlic

1 large or 2 medium-sized tomatoes

10 to 12 saffron threads

3 cups chicken stock

3 tablespoons olive oil

2 cups long-grain white rice

1 bay leaf

Salt, ground black pepper, and red pepper flakes

1 cup green peas (fresh or frozen)

1 jarred pimiento pepper

Chicken And Rice These two buddies travel together everywhere—Puerto Rico, Dominican Republic, Costa Rica, Cuba, South Carolina, Mexico, and far beyond the Americas' borders. It's usually the seasonings that make the difference from one national table to the next. Don't be intimidated if the names get complicated. It is simply chicken and rice cooked together.

Some barbecue aficionados are opposed to liquid smoke, while others, such as world-class talker and expert pitmaster Bobby Seale, dote on it.

Bobby Seale's Spicy Chicken Barbecue

To make the baste-marinade, squeeze enough juice from the lemons to yield ½ cup. Strain the juice into a saucepan to remove any seeds. Add the liquid smoke, vinegar, onion powder, Worcestershire sauce, and water. Place over high heat, stir well, and bring to a boil. Immediately remove from the heat. You should have about 4 cups.

To make the spicy chicken sauce, seed the jalapeño peppers, if desired, then chop finely. Place in a heavy saucepan. Add the V-8 Juice, Worcestershire sauce, liquid smoke, red pepper flakes, and 1 cup of the hickory-onion baste marinade. Stir well. Place over medium heat and bring to a gentle boil. Cover and boil gently over medium heat, stirring occasionally, until the flavors are well blended, about 25 minutes. Stir one last time, then remove from the heat. You should have about 4 cups.

Cut each chicken into quarters or eighths. Rinse the pieces and pat dry with paper towels. Place the chicken pieces in a large nonreactive pot or bowl (or in a plastic bag set in a rimmed container). Pour in 2 cups of the baste-marinade to immerse the chicken fully. Cover the pot or bowl or seal the plastic bag closed. Let stand for 2 hours at room temperature or for up to overnight in the refrigerator. Turn the chicken pieces occasionally as they marinate.

(continued on page 88)

Baste-marinade

About 3 lemons

⅓ cup pure hickory liquid smoke (see page 25)

½ cup red wine vinegar or cider vinegar

1 tablespoon onion powder

½ cup Worcestershire sauce

3 cups water

Reprinted by permission. (Ten Speed Press).

Bobby Seale's Spicy Chicken Barbecue (continued)

Sauce

- ⅓ cup fresh jalapeño peppers
- 3 cups V-8 Juice
- ⅓ cup Worcestershire sauce
- ⅓ cup pure hickory liquid smoke
- 1 tablespoon red pepper flakes
- 1 cup hickory-onion baste-marinade

- 2 chickens, 3 to 3 ½ pounds each
- 3 cups hickory wood chips
- Vegetable oil for grill rack

Place the hickory chips in a container and add the remaining 1 cup baste-marinade to them. Let soak for 30 minutes, then drain. Prepare a fire in a charcoal grill, using about 40 briquettes or so, and let them burn down to a white-ash-hot fire. Spread the briquettes out evenly, then spread the soaked chips over the briquettes. Let burn until the flames go out.

When the fire is ready, remove the chicken pieces from the marinade and drain well; reserve the marinade. Lightly rub the grill rack with oil and position it 4 to 6 inches above the fire. Place the chicken pieces on the grill rack and brush with the reserved marinade. Grill, turning frequently, until the chicken is nicely browned and no longer pink at the bone, about 50 minutes. During the last 10 minutes of cooking, stop basting with the marinade and instead brush the chicken pieces with the spicy chicken sauce 2 or 3 times. Alternatively, using tongs, dip the pieces into the sauce.

When the chicken pieces are ready, transfer them to a large platter and serve the remaining sauce on the side.

Serves 8

BBQ At The White House   When President Jimmy Carter was in office, I was invited to a barbecue at the White House. It was quite a sight. Right there on the White House lawns was a battery of spits and ovens turning out some truly memorable barbecue, and many of the cooks had been hard at work since dawn. The smells of grilled chicken, hot rolls and fruit pies wafted gloriously up and down Pennsylvania Avenue.

Although this West African dish is called groundnut stew, it is actually chicken in a groundnut—that is, peanut—sauce. I have used commercial peanut butter here, to speed up the preparation time, but you can also freshly grind your own roasted peanuts to a paste. This same sauce is good with meats, fish, and vegetables. Don't be stingy with the cayenne pepper! It needs the fiery accent. Serve the dish over rice.

Groundnut Stew

Rinse the chicken and pat dry with paper towels. Cut into serving pieces and season with salt and black pepper. Chop the onion, and peel and chop the tomatoes.

In a wide, heavy saucepan over medium heat, warm the oil. Add the chicken pieces and brown on all sides, 5 to 10 minutes. Using a slotted utensil, transfer the chicken pieces to a plate and set aside.

Add the onion to the oil remaining in the pan and saute over medium heat until softened, about 5 minutes. Stir in the tomatoes and cook briefly, then return the chicken to the pan. Pour in the chicken stock and add the cayenne pepper. Bring to a boil, reduce the heat to low, cover, and simmer until the chicken is nearly tender, about 30 minutes.

Ladle out about 1 cup of the cooking liquid into a bowl. Stir the peanut butter into it, and then stir the mixture into the pan. Taste and adjust the seasonings. Continue to simmer, stirring frequently to prevent sticking, until the chicken is fully tender and the flavors are blended, 10 to 15 minutes longer. Serve hot.

Serves 4

1 chicken, 2 ½ to 3 pounds

Salt and ground black pepper to taste

1 large yellow onion

4 tomatoes

3 tablespoons peanut oil

3 cups chicken stock

1 teaspoon cayenne pepper

½ cup chunky peanut butter

The Versatile Groundnut In West Africa, the groundnut, what most Americans know as the peanut, has myriad uses. It is cultivated as a source of cooking oil and flour and for eating for its own sake—simply salted, crushed into "butter," made into sauces and soups, fashioned into candies and desserts. This New World vine-like plant, which is actually a member of the bean family, takes its Old World name from the way it grows: its flower stalks dry, fall to the ground, and burrow beneath the soil, burying the emerging pods underground where they grow to maturity.

You may want to recalculate the math on how much chicken to buy for this dish. I believe that recipes are only guidelines, so the amount of chicken wings you need really depends on the number of people who will be sitting down to dinner – and how greedy they are.

Oven-fried Lemon Chicken Wings

4 pounds chicken wings

3 or 4 lemons

Garlic powder, onion powder, salt, and ground black pepper to taste

¼ cup butter

Rinse the chicken wings and pat dry with paper towels. Place in a large, shallow nonreactive dish or pan. Squeeze the juice from lemons; you should have about ½ cup. Drizzle the lemon juice over the wings and then season with the garlic and onion powders, salt, and pepper to taste. Turn the wings several times to coat well with the marinade, cover, and refrigerate overnight.

The next day, preheat an oven to 500 degrees F. Remove the wings from the marinade, reserving the marinade. Place the wings in a large roasting pan that will hold them in a single layer. Melt the butter and brush it evenly over the wings.

Place in the oven and cook for 10 minutes, turning once at the halfway point. The wings should begin to turn golden. Reduce the heat to 350 degrees F and pour the reserved marinade in the pan. Continue to cook, turning the wings and brushing with the pan juices every 10 minutes, until golden brown and crisp, about 30 minutes longer. Serve hot or at room temperature.

Serves 6

In Praise Of Chicken Wings I love chicken wings. I know a lot of people think they're too bony, but that's what I like about them. All those bones carry the best flavor. I also never cut off the wing tips – they're the tastiest part. While the drumettes are being served at fancy cocktail parties, the wing tips are being packaged for sale in low-end supermarkets. But then maybe you can't trust me. I am also one of those folks who like the last piece over the fence.

The guinea hen, a West African fowl that gained favor during America's early colonial days, is gamey and lean, and easily dries out during cooking. I lard the hens with bacon to keep them moist. Fresh guinea hens are difficult to locate, but frozen ones can be found in many poultry shops and sometimes in supermarkets.

Braised Guinea Hen

1 guinea hen, about 3 ½ pounds

Butter

Salt, black pepper, and cayenne pepper to taste

1 yellow onion

1 celery stalk

4 fresh thyme sprigs or ½ teaspoon dried thyme

3 or 4 slices bacon

1 cup chicken stock or water

Preheat an oven to 350 degrees F.

Rinse the guinea hen and pat dry with paper towels. Split the bird in half. Rub the skin with butter and season with salt and black and cayenne peppers.

Thinly slice the onion and cut the celery stalk into 4 to 6 pieces. Scatter half of the onion and celery over the bottom of a heavy ovenproof pot large enough to hold the guinea hen in a single layer. Place the guinea hen, skin side up, in the pot and poke the thyme sprigs in around the breasts and wings (or sprinkle on the dried thyme). Lay the bacon slices over the hen and scatter the remaining onion and celery on top. Pour in the stock or water.

Cover and place in the oven. Cook, basting often with the pan juices, until the hen is done, 1½ to 2 hours. To test, pierce the thickest part of the thigh; the juices should run clear.

To serve, carve into serving pieces and place on a platter. Spoon the pan juices over the top. Serves 4

The Labors Of Hercules George and Martha Washington often entertained, and they relied on their accomplished cook, a slave named Hercules, to prepare the lavish feasts such occasions demanded. Indeed, so respected was Hercules's culinary skills, that when the government moved to Philadelphia, the president immediately sent for Hercules. The City of Brotherly Love made a great impression on its new resident, but Hercules soon found himself being shipped back to Virginia, a fact that had nothing to do with how well he did his job and everything to do with a Pennsylvania law that granted slaves their freedom after six months of residence. Washington, not wanting to lose his prize cook, would regularly send Hercules back to Virginia just before six months were up, only to have him returned to his household soon after. At the end of his administration, when Washington was returning to Virginia for good, Hercules came up missing, never to be found again.

Just like Hoppin' John (see page 102), there are those who prefer jambalaya as a sauce spooned over rice—some folks call it the "big sauce"—while others, including me, like it all cooked together. To my mind, the great jambalayas are wet but never soupy. I have made this dish from leftover chicken, but you can always start fresh.

Jambalaya

Chop the chicken and the ham into bite-sized pieces; you should have about 1½ cups of each. Cut the sausages into ½-inch-thick slices. Seed the bell pepper, then chop the bell pepper, yellow onion, garlic, and the scallions, including the tender green tops. Peel and chop the tomatoes.

In a large, heavy skillet over medium heat, warm the vegetable oil. Add the ham and sausage and sauté until well browned, 7 to 10 minutes. Add the flour, stir well, and add the bell pepper, yellow onion, garlic, and scallions and saute until softened, about 5 minutes. Add the tomatoes, thyme, cumin, allspice, bay leaves, salt, black and cayenne peppers, and chicken and mix well. Then stir in the rice and pour in the stock. The liquid should just cover the contents of the skillet. Bring to a boil, cover, reduce the heat to low, and cook until the rice is tender, about 20 minutes.

To serve, remove and discard the bay leaf. Spoon the rice and meats onto a platter.

Serves 6 to 8

½ pound cooked chicken meat

½ pound cooked ham

1 pound smoked sausages

1 small green bell pepper

1 large yellow onion

3 cloves garlic

5 scallions

3 large tomatoes

¼ cup vegetable oil

2 tablespoons all-purpose flour

½ teaspoon dried thyme

½ teaspoon ground cumin

½ teaspoon ground allspice

2 bay leaves

Salt, ground black pepper, and cayenne pepper to taste

2 cups long-grain white rice

3 cups chicken, beef, or vegetable stock, or as needed

Word Games Nothing is more Creole than jambalaya. According to some food historians, the name has been cobbled together from the French la and jambon. Others insist it is from the Spanish jamón and that the ya is a West African word meaning "rice." I suspect it is a blend of all of them, and maybe some we haven't even identified yet—a true Creole dish.

The size of the roast you buy will depend on the number of people you are feeding, whether or not they are serious meat eaters, and if you plan to serve a sit-down or buffet meal. The latter is particularly important to the decision. I've known people who claim they eat very little meat, but who then really load up their plates at a buffet table. A crown roast is an elegant, showy, pricy cut, so I suggest you reserve it for a sit-down affair and allow two ribs per person.

Ask your butcher to remove the backbone and secure the ribs in a circle. You can cap the ribs with those little paper frills if you like, or even decorate with crabapples. The hollow of the pork roast will not hold all of the stuffing—or "dressing" as we call it in the South Carolina Low Country. You will have enough for the roast and an extra panful.

Crown Pork Roast with Sage-Apple Cornbread Stuffing

1 pork crown roast, about 6 pounds (12 ribs)

Salt, ground black pepper, and garlic powder to taste

Preheat an oven to 400 degrees F.

Season the crown roast with salt, black pepper, and garlic powder, rubbing them in thoroughly over all the surfaces of the roast. Place the roast in a roasting pan with the ribs facing upward. Roast for 30 minutes.

Meanwhile, make the stuffing: Mince the celery. Chop the onions. Peel, core and quarter the apples. Chop the sage; you should have about ¼ cup.

Place the apples and cornbread cubes in a large bowl. In a large skillet over medium heat, melt half of the butter. Add the celery and onions and saute until they begin to soften, about 3 minutes. Add the contents of the skillet to the apples and cornbread.

Melt the remaining butter and add to the bowl along with the sage, thyme, and poultry seasoning. Stir and toss with a fork or wooden spoon to mix well. Add the stock and mix until all the ingredients are evenly moistened.

When the meat has been in the oven for 30 minutes, remove the pan to a countertop. Spoon some of the stuffing into the hollow, mounding it slightly. Cover the filling with aluminum foil. Grease a baking dish and spoon the remaining stuffing into it.

Reduce the oven temperature 350 degrees F. Return the roast to the oven and slip the dish of stuffing into the oven as well, putting it on another rack if necessary. Continue to roast for 1 hour longer, then remove the foil covering the stuffing and roast for a final 15 minutes, or until the meat is tender but still quite moist when pierced.

Transfer the roast to a large platter and cover loosely with foil. Let rest for 20 minutes.

To serve, spoon the stuffing out of the center, then carve by slicing between the bones to remove the chops one at a time. Serve the dish of stuffing on the side.

Serves 6

Stuffing

- 2 celery stalks
- 1 yellow onion
- 2 tart apples
-   Small bunch of fresh sage
- 4 cups dry cornbread cubes
- ¼ cup butter
- ¼ teaspoon dried thyme
- 1 teaspoon poultry seasoning
- 1 cup chicken stock

A Special Dinner The last time I made this pork roast was in February of 1965. I was having a dinner party and my dear friend Larry Neal was one of the invited guests. Everyone on the list was special to me, so I splurged for this expensive cut of meat. When the roast came out of the oven it was beautiful, but Larry had still not arrived. Then the phone rang. It was Larry, and he spoke only three words: "Malcolm's been shot."

This succulent roast, studded with garlic, is great with boiled yuca as an accompaniment. Kali is my oldest daughter. Her sister, Chandra, became a mother before she did, and Kali was crazy about her little nephew, Oscar. Oscar was—and is—crazy about his Auntie Kali, too. Indeed, he caused some real sibling rivalry when he was small by going on about what a great cook Auntie Kali was. This is one of her celebrated dishes.

Auntie Kali's Puerto Rican-style Pork Roast

Rinse the pork with vinegar and water and drain well. Place in a shallow dish. Squeeze the juice from the limes and pour it over the roast. Let stand at room temperature for 1 hour.

Preheat an oven to 450 degrees F. Chop 3 of the garlic cloves or enough to measure 1 tablespoon. Place in a small bowl and add the onion powder, sage, rosemary, basil, and thyme and mix well. Rub the pork with olive oil and then rub the herb mixture over it, coating evenly. Cut the remaining 1 or 2 garlic cloves into small slivers. Using the tip of a sharp knife, pierce the pork roast in several places on all sides and slip the pieces of garlic into the incisions. Dust the pork with flour, again coating evenly.

Pour a little olive oil into a heavy roasting pan and place the pan in the oven to heat for about 10 minutes. (It has to be a heavy pan or the meat won't sear properly when it is added.) Remove the pan from the oven, place the pork in it, and turn the pork to sear on all sides in the hot oil. Place the roast fat side up in the pan and return it to the oven. Reduce the oven temperature to 325 degrees F and roast until tender, about 1 ½ hours. Remove the roast from the oven and let rest for 15 minutes before carving.

Serves 6

1   bone-in pork shoulder roast, about 4 pounds

Distilled white vinegar diluted with water

2   limes

4   or 5 cloves garlic

1   tablespoon onion powder

1   tablespoon dried sage

1   tablespoon dried rosemary

1   tablespoon dried basil

1   tablespoon dried thyme

Olive oil

All-purpose flour

About Yuca Almost every Caribbean island claims some version of this pork roast, and yuca is often its partner on the plate. Yuca, a tropical root, is believed to have been first domesticated in the Amazon basin. It has rough, brown skin and starchy white flesh and can be found in Latin American and Caribbean markets both fresh and frozen. Just peel it and boil it in plenty of water until it's tender, then serve doused with minced garlic and olive oil.

Beg, borrow, or steal a smoker if you don't have one, because a smoker is absolutely necessary for this tasty beef brisket. Serve it with Old-fashioned Coleslaw (page 51), grilled eggplant and zucchini, Southern Pasta & Bean Salad (page 41), and Classic White Potato Salad (page 55).

Barbecued Beef Brisket with Dry Rub

Dry Rub

- 2 tablespoons dried thyme
- 2 tablespoons onion powder
- 2 tablespoons hot Hungarian paprika
- 2 tablespoons garlic powder
- 2 tablespoons kosher salt
- 2 tablespoons ground black pepper
- 2 tablespoons dried oregano
- 2 teaspoons ground cumin
- 1 teaspoon dry mustard

- 1 beef brisket, about 5 pounds
- 1 can (12 ounces) beer

To make the dry rub, combine the thyme, onion powder, paprika, garlic powder, kosher salt, black pepper, oregano, cumin, and mustard in a bowl. Stir until all the ingredients are evenly distributed.

Place the beef brisket in a shallow nonreactive pan or dish. Smear the rub evenly over the surface of the meat. Cover and refrigerate for 2 hours.

Fire up the smoker according to the manufacturer's instructions, using your favorite wood chips. Place the brisket fat side down in the smoker, close the cover, and cook for 3 hours.

Remove the brisket from the smoker and place it on a large sheet of heavy-duty aluminum foil. Douse the brisket with the beer, seal together the edges of the foil and return it to the smoker. Re-cover the smoker and cook until the meat is fork tender, about 2 hours longer.

Remove from the smoker, unwrap, and let rest for about 10 minutes, then slice on the diagonal and serve.

Serves 8 to 10

Barbecue Tales Great barbecue stories are told and retold all over the United States. I read about a guy who couldn't pay his restaurant bill and left a sauce recipe instead, with a note saying it had come to him from God. Or the one about the night prowler at a barbecue joint in North Carolina. He had tried to hide in a vat of pepper vinegar so the police wouldn't catch him. Boy was he pink and pickled! And if there is any doubt that this country is barbecue crazy, just keep in mind that a Barbecue Barbie with her own special grill was put on the market in 1951.

This recipe is adapted from a recipe from Enid Donaldson, a celebrated Jamaican food writer and cook. She writes that there are more goats in Jamaica than sheep, making goat meat a favorite. The recipe calls for boneless meat, but you can use bone-in if you like; I prefer to mix the two because the bones impart flavor. Serve this robust curry over boiled plantains or rice.

Jamaican Curried Goat

Cut the goat or lamb into 1½-inch cubes. Place in a shallow nonreactive dish or pan.

Break apart the cloves in the head of garlic, peel them, and place in a blender. Coarsely chop the scallion and add it to the blender along with the cayenne pepper, salt, curry powder and wine vinegar. Process until smooth.

Pour the curry mixture over the meat, turn the pieces to coat evenly, cover, and refrigerate for a few hours or as long as overnight.

Remove the goat meat from the marinade and pat dry with paper towels; reserve the marinade. In a large, heavy skillet over medium heat, warm the vegetable oil. Working in batches if necessary, add the goat or lamb pieces and brown well on all sides, 5 to 10 minutes.

Pour in the water, scraping up any browned bits. Add the reserved marinade and mix well. Cover, reduce the heat to low, and simmer until the meat is fork tender, 1½ to 2 hours for the goat or 1 to 1½ hours for the lamb. (If you are using bone-in goat, it may take up to an hour longer.) Taste and adjust the seasonings, then serve.

Serves 6 to 8

3 pounds boneless goat or lamb, or part bone-in meat

1 head garlic

1 scallion

½ teaspoon cayenne pepper

1 teaspoon salt

¼ cup curry powder

½ cup white or red wine vinegar

2 tablespoons vegetable oil

2 cups water

A Kingston Market When I visited Enid Donaldson in Jamaica, she guided me through a colorful marketplace in Kingston. Shopping with her was a wonderful experience. We gathered breadfruit, yuca, and spices, and then went back to her kitchen to prepare a tableful of traditional Jamaican party dishes. When Jamaicans are having a party, curried goat is always on the menu. In fact, if there is no goat, it is not considered a party.

This is a relative of Hoppin' John (page 102), made with my favorite vegetable, okra, which is what gives Susan the "limp."

Limpin' Susan

Seed the bell pepper. Mince the bell pepper, onion, and garlic. Cut the okra into ¼-inch-thick rounds. Peel the shrimp. Make a shallow incision along the back of each shrimp and lift out and discard the vein-like tract.

In a large skillet over medium heat, warm the oil. Add the onion and pepper and sauté until softened, about 5 minutes. Add the garlic and sauté for 2 minutes to release its flavor. Add the rice, stir well until the grains are coated, and cook, stirring often, until opaque, 3 to 4 minutes. Add the okra, stock, salt, and black and cayenne peppers. Bring to a boil, reduce the heat to low, cover, and cook until the rice is tender and the liquid has been absorbed, about 20 minutes.

Taste and adjust the seasonings. Stir in the shrimp and cook until the shrimp curl and turn pink, 5 to 8 minutes. Transfer to a bowl and serve.

Serves 4

- ½ small green bell pepper
- ½ small yellow onion
- 3 cloves garlic
- 1 pound okra
- 1 pound medium-sized shrimp
- 3 tablespoons vegetable oil
- 1 cup long-grain white rice
- 2 cup chicken stock
- 1 teaspoon salt

Ground black pepper and cayenne pepper to taste

The Okra Trail Okra first traveled to the New World during the early years of the slave trade. Today in Brazil, members of Condomblé, an Afro-Brazilian religion that made the same journey four centuries ago, include a dish built around okra in their religious observances. Its preparation calls for a ritualistic cutting of the pods that is both precise and time-consuming. In the South, okra shows up in many a pot of gumbo (see page 80), as well as in countless other dishes, from Real Southern Succotash (page 130) to a variety of coastal soups.

For some people, hoppin' John is peas and rice cooked together. For others, it's the peas over the rice. It doesn't matter. Anytime a black-eyed pea meets a grain of rice, it becomes hoppin' John.

Hoppin' John

2½ cups (1 pound) dried black-eyed peas

1 pound smoke sausages

8 cups stock, any kind

Salt, ground black pepper, garlic powder, and red pepper flakes to taste

Proper Geechee Rice (page 134)

Pick over the black-eyed peas, discarding any misshapen peas or grit and rinse in cold water. Place in a large bowl with water to cover generously. Let soak overnight.

The next day, cut the sausages into slices about ½ inch thick. In a large, heavy saucepan over medium heat, saute the sausages until nicely browned, 5 to 10 minutes. (You probably won't need any oil, as the sausages give off their own.) Drain the peas and add to the saucepan along with the stock. Season with the salt, black pepper, garlic powder, and red pepper flakes. Bring to a boil, reduce the heat to low, and simmer, uncovered, until tender, 1 to 1½ hours.

About 30 minutes before the beans are ready, cook the rice. When the beans and rice are ready, spoon the rice into individual bowls and top with the black-eyed peas.

Serves 6 to 8

Who was Hoppin' John? Just exactly who was John? The answer depends on whom you talk to and what you read. Some say John was a servant who made a dish of black-eyed peas and rice that was so good, everyone asked for seconds. That meant he had to keep hopping around the table to accommodate his diners. Others insist that children would hop around the table in anticipation of John's great creation. And still others say that the name comes from the sound the peas make as they pop and hop around the pan.

I was having some people over for dinner and intended to make a paella. I fooled around, though, and by the time I got to the fish market, it was closed. But because I believe that cooking is like jazz, that you can always improvise, I went home, looked at my shelf, and came up with this most delicious dish. And the meat eaters loved it, too.

Gullah Vegetable Paella

Chop the yellow onion and the scallions, including the tender green tops. Seed and chop the bell pepper, and mince the garlic. Trim the ends of the green beans and cut into 1½-inch lengths. (To save time, use about 1½ cups frozen cut-up green beans.) Peel the carrot and dice it. Rinse the black beans and drain well. Crumble the saffron threads into ½ cup of the stock.

Preheat an oven to 350 degrees F.

In a heavy ovenproof saucepan over medium heat, warm the vegetable oil. Add the yellow onion, bell pepper, and garlic and saute until beginning to soften, just a few minutes.

Add the scallions and continue to saute for another minute. Then stir in the carrot, green beans and black beans and saute, stirring constantly, for 1 minute.

Add the rice and season with salt and black and cayenne peppers. Stir until well combined. Pour in 1½ cups of the chicken stock and the saffron and its soaking water, raise the heat to high, and bring to a boil.

(continued on page 105)

1 small yellow onion

3 scallions

½ green bell pepper

2 cloves garlic

¼ pound green beans

1 carrot

½ cup drained canned black beans

10 to 12 saffron threads

2 to 2¼ cups chicken stock

3 tablespoons vegetable oil

1 cup long-grain white rice

Salt, ground black pepper, and cayenne pepper to taste

1 cup green peas (fresh or frozen)

Gullah Vegetable Paella (continued)

Remove from the heat, cover with a tight-fitting lid, and place in the oven. Bake until the rice is tender and the liquid is absorbed, about 20 minutes. If all of the liquid is gone and the rice is still not tender, sprinkle with the remaining ¼ cup stock, re-cover and return to the oven until the rice is cooked.

Remove from the oven and stir in the peas. Re-cover the pan and return to the oven until the peas are tender, about 5 minutes.

Remove from the oven and let rest for 10 minutes before serving.

Serves 4

Paella We can taste the Spanish influence in many preparations throughout the Americas. My favorite of these is paella, a glorious dish that allows the cook great freedom of culinary expression. One can use just about any ingredient on hand, from vegetables and seafood to sausages and chicken.

There are several tales as to how paella got its name. One claims the dish was prepared when a Spanish princess paid an unexpected visit to a commoner's country inn. Faced with a royal challenge, the clever innkeeper made a pilaf of "on hand" ingredients, flavored it with saffron, and said it was para ella, Spanish for "for her." Another story involves a Spanish king, somewhat of a foodie and a womanizer who was known for his great late-night suppers in the palace apartments. He would make an elaborate rice dish (or have his cook do it) and when asked for whom such a special dish had been created, he would point to his latest and say para ella.

This dish uses all the classic pantry items of the South Carolina Low Country. It is a meant for a crowd, to be enjoyed when family and friends come together.

Saint Helena Stew

6 quarts water

⅓ cup favorite crab boil

5 large boiling potatoes

1½ pounds smoked sausages

6 ears of corn

2 pounds large shrimp in the shell

Favorite hot-pepper sauce

In a large stockpot, combine the water and crab boil and bring to a boil over high heat.

Meanwhile, peel and quarter the potatoes. Cut the sausages into 2-inch-long pieces. Break or cut the ears of corn in half. Rinse the shrimp but do not peel.

Add the potatoes to the stockpot, reduce the heat to medium, and cook, uncovered, for 10 minutes. Then add the corn and cook for 10 minutes. Finally, add the shrimp and cook until they curl and turn pink, 5 to 8 minutes longer.

Using a slotted spoon, remove the potatoes, sausages, corn, and shrimp to a platter. Serve hot--and don't forget the hot sauce.

Serves 6

Saint Helena Island You might know this dish as Low Country boil, Beaufort stew, or even Frogmore stew. Frogmore was the name of a plantation on Saint Helena Island, and it was also the name given to the island's town center, a general store and post office on Highway 21. But not all the people of this South Carolina Sea Island liked being called Frogmoreans. Rich in history, this is the island where Penn School, the first school in the South for freed blacks, was established in 1862. For years, the island residents fought to get the post office name changed from Frogmore, an old plantation name, to Saint Helena. And when these same people made this dish, they bristled when anyone ever called it Frogmore stew. In 1981, the post office officially became known as Saint Helena Island Post Office, and I call this dish Saint Helena Stew in honor of that victory. If you are lucky, you will eat it at a picnic table under the moss-hung oak trees of South Carolina.

Here I have used vegetables to create a delectable, healthful gumbo that both vegetarians and nonvegetarians will appreciate. I serve it over white rice, but it would be good over brown rice, too.

Vegetable Gumbo

Chop the onion and celery. Seed and chop the red, yellow, and green bell peppers; you should have about 1 cup chopped bell pepper. Mince the garlic. Chop the scallions, including the tender green tops.

Open the can of tomatoes and drain them. Chop the tomatoes. Chop the parsley. Core the cabbage and chop the leaves; you should have about 1 cup. Remove and discard any tough stems from the collards and chop the leaves; you should have about 1 cup.

In a large frying pan over medium heat, warm the olive oil. Add the onion, celery, all the bell peppers, garlic, and scallions and saute until softened, about 8 minutes. Add the tomatoes, parsley, thyme, salt, and black and cayenne peppers and stir well. Add the chopped cabbage and collards and pour in the stock. Bring to a boil, reduce the heat to low, and simmer, uncovered, until the vegetables are very tender and the flavors are blended, about 45 minutes.

About 30 minutes before the gumbo is ready, cook the rice.

To serve, place the rice into individual shallow soup plates and spoon the gumbo over and around it.

Serves 4 to 6

1 yellow onion

1 large celery stalk

½ red bell pepper

½ yellow bell pepper

½ green bell pepper

2 cloves garlic

2 scallions

1 can (16 ounces) canned tomatoes

4 or 5 fresh parsley sprigs

¼ small green cabbage

4 to 6 collard leaves (note: collard greens)

2 tablespoons olive oil

4 cups vegetable stock

Dried thyme, salt, ground black pepper, and cayenne pepper to taste

Proper Geechee Rice (page 134)

Gumbo Z' herbes   Creole cooks in New Orleans are famous for a gumbo made from just greens and herbs. It's called gumbo z̄'herbes or gumbo aux herbes, and, according to legend, was created long ago for the Good Friday table. Today, it is still believed that if you eat a gumbo made from seven greens and meet seven people on Good Friday, you will enjoy good fortune for the next twelve months.

Food historians tend to agree that Thomas Jefferson was the only gourmet ever to hold the highest office in the land. Records show that macaroni and cheese was served at his Monticello estate, a residence that was renowned for its opulent spreads.

Monticello Macaroni & Cheese

8 to 10 ounces sharp Cheddar cheese

½ small green bell pepper

2 eggs

7 ounces macaroni

¼ cup butter

2 cups evaporated milk, half-and-half, or heavy cream

1 teaspoon salt

½ teaspoon ground white pepper

Finely shred the Cheddar cheese; you should have 2 ½ cups. Set aside. Seed and finely chop the bell pepper. In a small bowl, lightly beat the eggs until blended.

Preheat an oven to 350 degrees F. Grease a 9-by-13-inch baking dish with butter.

Bring a large saucepan of salted water to a boil. Add the macaroni and boil until just tender, about 10 minutes. Do not overcook the macaroni as it will cook further in the oven. Drain and place in a large bowl.

Add 3 tablespoons of the butter, 2 cups of the cheese, the bell pepper, eggs, milk, salt, and pepper to the macaroni. Stir until well mixed. Transfer to the prepared baking dish. Sprinkle the remaining ½ cup cheese evenly over the casserole. Cut the remaining 1 tablespoon butter into bits and scatter the bits over the cheese.

Bake until the top is golden brown, about 30 minutes. Remove from the oven and let cool slightly before serving.

Serves 6

Isaac's Story Even though Thomas Jefferson was a well-known food snob, he wasn't a cook. According to a slave named Isaac, who worked in the house at Monticello, the only time Jefferson ever came into the kitchen was to wind the clock. Everybody who was anybody dined at the estate, and, again according to Isaac, diners never sat down to fewer than eight courses. When Jefferson went to France as a diplomat in 1784, he took along one of his slaves, James Hemmings, and sent him to cooking school in Paris.

Side Dishes

Do you like potato chips? Plantain chips? If the answer is yes to either or both questions, you'll love yam chips, a.k.a. sweet potato chips. I promise you that you won't be able to eat just one.

Southern-fried Louisiana Yam Chips

4 yams (sweet potatoes)

Vegetable shortening for deep frying

Salt

Peel the yams and cut crosswise into very thin slices. Place in a large bowl, add water to cover, and refrigerate overnight. (The soaking removes the excess starch.)

The next day, in a large, deep skillet (or in a deep-fat fryer), melt shortening to a depth of 2 to 3 inches and heat to 365 degrees F on a deep-fat thermometer. Drain the yams and pat dry with paper towels.

Working with about one-third of the yam slices at a time, slip the slices into the hot shortening. Fry, turning as needed to cook evenly, until golden brown, 5 to 8 minutes. Using a slotted spoon, transfer to paper towels to drain briefly, then place on a platter and sprinkle with salt. Serve hot.

Serves 4 to 6

Yam Seasonings The Louisiana Yam Commission is quick to point out just how versatile their beloved yam can be. In a list of possible seasonings for yam chips, they include the following savory and sweet possibilities: celery salt, onion salt, garlic salt, salt and cayenne pepper, confectioners' sugar, cinnamon sugar, or a mixture of confectioners' sugar and minced candied orange peel.

If you can't find African yams, have patience. They came to my supermarket. One day while shopping, I saw two African women carrying huge tin foil pans. I figured that the deli department had catered something for them. But then I saw them setting up a table and it turned out they were promoting African yams, which the market had decided to stock. I sampled their dishes and then came up with my own. So, again, be patient. African yams will eventually come to your market. As folks say, "Soon come."

Supermarket African Yams with Tomato Gravy

To make the tomato gravy, seed the bell pepper and cut up. Chop the onion. Peel and chop the tomato. Transfer the tomato paste to a good-sized pitcher and slowly stir in enough of the water to make a sauce with the consistency of cream.

In a skillet over medium-high heat, warm the vegetable (or other) oil. Add half of the onion, the curry powder, cayenne, and nutmeg and saute until browned, about 10 minutes. Meanwhile, place the remaining onion, the bell pepper, and the tomato in a blender and process until nicely chopped.

When the onion in the skillet is nicely browned, add the contents of the blender and the diluted tomato paste and reduce the heat to medium. Simmer, uncovered, until the vegetables are tender and the flavors have blended, about 15 minutes. Season with salt.

Meanwhile, bring a large saucepan filled with water to a rapid boil. Peel the yams, then rinse well under cold running water. Cut crosswise into 1½-inch-thick slices. Add to the rapidly boiling water and boil until tender, about 10 minutes. About 2 minutes before the yams are ready, add salt to the water.

Drain the yams, and transfer to a serving bowl. Pour the sauce into a separate bowl and pass at the table.

Serves 4 to 6

Gravy

- ½ green bell pepper
- 1 yellow onion
- 1 tomato
- 1 can (6 ounces) tomato paste
- 1½ to 2 cups water
- ¼ cup vegetable, corn, canola or olive oil
- ½ teaspoon curry powder
- ½ teaspoon cayenne pepper
- Dash of ground nutmeg
- Salt to taste

- 2 pounds African yams
- Salt to taste

This recipe comes from Mama Rosa's restaurant in Philadelphia. Mama Rosa is my cousin. She and her husband, Walter ("Doc"), started out with a van from which they served hot dinners to workers on construction sites, saving them from eating cold sandwiches all the time. From those beginnings was born the restaurant motto: People want real food and Mama Rosa's delivers.

Mama Rosa's Gingered Yam & Apple Bake

3 yams (sweet potatoes)

2 large red apples

¼ cup unsalted butter

Salt, ground nutmeg, ground cinnamon, and ground ginger to taste

1 cup apple juice

Scrub the yams but do not peel. Bring a large saucepan filled with water to a boil, add the yams, and boil until barely tender, about 20 minutes, depending on their size. Drain well and, when cool enough to handle, peel off the skins. Cut the yams crosswise into ¼-inch-thick slices. Peel, halve, and core the apples. Cut into slices.

Preheat an oven to 325 degrees F. Grease a 9-by-13-inch baking dish with a little of the butter.

Layer half of the yam slices in the baking dish, overlapping them slightly. Top with half of the apple slices. Sprinkle with salt, nutmeg, cinnamon, and ginger. Cut the remaining butter into small bits and use half of it to dot the surface. Repeat procedure and pour the apple juice evenly over the surface.

Bake, uncovered, until the apples and yams are tender when pierced with a fork and the top is nicely golden, about 20 minutes. As the dish bakes, redistribute the juices to moisten any areas that are dry.

Serves 6

Yams vs. Sweet Potatoes True yams are tuberous roots, but they are botanically distinct from the American sweet potato. Some food scholars believe the English word "yam" is derived from the African "nyam." They suggest that when the African slaves were brought to the New World and saw native American tubers similar to those in their homeland, they said what sounded like "yams," and the name stuck. I like that story, true or not, because in the South Carolina Low Country we use the word "nyam," meaning "to eat." In the flash of a pan, a Gullah person will say "yenna come nyam at my house" - "come over and eat."

Serve this rich, delectable dish alongside a holiday turkey, or anytime you want a special accompaniment.

Candied Sweet Potatoes

4 sweet potatoes

2 cups pineapple juice

½ cup firmly packed brown sugar

½ cup unsweetened canned coconut milk

Ground cinnamon, ground nutmeg, and ground mace to taste

½ cup butter

Scrub the sweet potatoes but do not peel. Bring a large pot of water to a boil. Add the sweet potatoes and boil until barely tender, 15 to 20 minutes; they should be firm. Drain well, let cool, peel, and cut into ¼-inch-thick slices.

When you put the sweet potatoes on to cook, in a separate heavy pan, combine the pineapple juice, brown sugar, and coconut milk. Bring to a boil, stirring to dissolve the sugar. Reduce the heat to medium and simmer, stirring occasionally, until thickened slightly, 15 to 20 minutes. Remove from the heat.

Preheat an oven to 350 degrees F. Grease a 9-inch square baking dish with butter. Make a layer of sweet potato slices in the prepared baking dish, overlapping the slices slightly. Sprinkle with cinnamon, nutmeg, and mace. Repeat the layering and seasoning until all the sweet potato slices have been used. Pour the pineapple juice syrup evenly over the top. Melt the butter and drizzle it evenly over the top as well.

Bake until the sweet potatoes are tender when pierced with a fork and the top is golden, 40 to 45 minutes. As the dish bakes, using a large spoon, redistribute the juices to moisten any areas that are dry. Serve hot directly from the dish.

Serves 4 to 6

Sweet Potato Vines This idea will sound familiar to anyone who has tried to grow a house plant from an avocado pit. It comes from the national Sweet Potato Council with promises of it being foolproof: use a jar with an opening that will eventually support a sweet potato vine. Place the sweet potato in the jar, narrow end down. Fill the jar with water, immersing the sweet potato, and put the jar in a warm, dark place. New roots should start to grow in a few days, and the stem should appear in about 10 days. As soon as this happens, shift the jar to a sunny window. As the vine grows, it can be left to trail or trained to climb.

I'm going to tell you what the devil do despise . . . the natural truth. My paternal grandmother, Estella Smart—Mother Dear, as I called her—made the best sweet potato pone in the whole world. This old-timey recipe, which is also a good dessert, is based on my memory of her extraordinary version. Try this one. It can't fail to be good.

Mother Dear's Sweet Potato Pone

Preheat an oven to 350 degrees F. Grease a 9-by-5-inch loaf pan with butter.

Peel the sweet potatoes. Finely grate them into a large bowl; you should have about 2 ½ cups. Melt the butter.

Add the sugar, evaporated milk, and melted butter to the grated sweet potato and mix well. Then stir in the allspice, cinnamon, cloves, nutmeg, and salt until evenly distributed. Finally, mix in the vanilla extract.

Transfer the sweet potato mixture to the prepared pan, smoothing the top. Bake until the mixture is firm and golden, 50 to 60 minutes. Serve hot directly from the dish.

Serves 6 to 8

3 sweet potatoes

¾ sugar

½ cup evaporated milk

¼ cup melted butter

½ teaspoon ground allspice

½ teaspoon ground cinnamon

½ teaspoon ground cloves

½ teaspoon ground nutmeg

Dash of salt

1 teaspoon vanilla extract

Mother Dear Estella Smart was not an over-the-hill-and-through-the-woods-to-grandmother's-house-we-go kind of grandmother. I never had a sit-down dinner at her house. She could cook, but she never cooked for us, her grandchildren. When we went to visit her, we had to bring a bag lunch, except sometimes we would get lucky and she would make something. I think I remember everything I ever ate at her house: biscuits so light it was as if they had wings, fresh-churned peach ice cream, spring turnip greens with dumplings, and sweet potato pone. Estella Smart did not pass on any culinary wisdom, but she did influence my life greatly in every other way.

You will need to cut the sweet potatoes lengthwise for this recipe, so choose uniformly shaped ones to make the task easier.

Oven-fried Sweet Potatoes

4 sweet potatoes

Peanut oil

Salt and ground cumin to taste

Preheat an oven to 350 degrees F.

Peel the sweet potatoes. Cut each sweet potato lengthwise into slices ⅓ inch thick. Place the potato slices in a shallow bowl and sprinkle with peanut oil. Turn the slices in the bowl to coat them evenly with the oil, then sprinkle with salt and cumin.

Transfer the sweet potato slices to a baking sheet, arranging them in a single layer. Bake until tender when pierced with a fork, 30 to 40 minutes. Serve piping hot from the oven.

Serves 4 to 6

The Versatile Sweet Potato The white potato has nothing on the sweet potato when it comes to versatility. Sweet potatoes can be french fried, made into chips (see page 112), panfried, or baked. For a special breakfast, try home-fried sweet potatoes, which are particularly tasty alongside scrapple or a slice of country ham. For a special supper side dish, thread cubes of parboiled and chilled sweet potato and pineapple onto skewers, brush with a mixture of pineapple juice and honey, and broil or grill. Or just scrub and dry the sweet potatoes well, rub with a little oil, and bake in a 350 degree F oven until tender. The cooking time depends on the size; they should be tender to the touch (use an oven mitt).

I say "mashed potatoes" and you are probably thinking white potatoes. But sweet potatoes are wonderful mashed and seasoned with orange juice and spices.

Side Dishes **119**

Mashed Sweet Potatoes with Honey & Spices

Scrub the sweet potatoes but do not peel. Bring a large pot of water to a boil. Add the sweet potatoes and boil until tender, about 40 minutes.

Meanwhile, preheat an oven to 375 degrees F. Select a baking dish large enough to accommodate the sweet potatoes once they are mashed and grease it with butter.

Drain the sweet potatoes and, when just cool enough to handle, peel and place in a bowl. Melt the butter. Using a potato masher, mash the sweet potatoes while adding the melted butter and ½ cup orange juice. Season with the honey, salt, nutmeg and mace. If the mixture seems a little too stiff, add more orange juice.

Transfer to a baking dish and, using a large spoon, swirl the mixture to form several peaks on the surface. Bake until the peaks are browned, about 15 minutes. Serve hot directly from the dish.

Serves 6

4 sweet potatoes

¼ cup butter (or less if you prefer)

½ cup orange juice, or as needed

¼ cup honey

Pinch of salt

Dash of ground nutmeg

Dash of ground mace

Sweet Potato History After Columbus' first voyage to the New World, he took the sweet potato back to Spain, where it was literally eaten up. It wasn't long before the rest of Europe was growing and cooking the delicious vegetable as well. They called it a Spanish potato to distinguish it from the white (or Irish) potato. Nearly a century ago, George Washington Carver recorded 118 different uses for the nutritious sweet potato. Today, in the same brick building at Tuskegee Institute where Dr. Carver did his research, scientists are trying to develop a way to grow these extraordinary plants on the moon.

I make this sprightly salsa for spooning over everything from greens to rice to a grilled chop to fried eggplant. Although the onions are the stars here, the tomatoes are more than simply bit players, so only sweet, vine-ripened ones will do.

Three-Onion Salsa

Chop all of the onions and place in a bowl. Add the vinegar and set aside for 2 hours to marinate.

Meanwhile, chop the tomatoes and place in a another bowl. When the onions have finished marinating, drain them and add to the tomatoes, along with the oregano (chopped, if using fresh), salt, cumin, and red pepper flakes. Stir well, cover, and refrigerate for at least 1 hour (but not longer than 3 hours) to allow the flavors to marry.

Bring to room temperature before serving with grilled vegetables, meat or fish.

Makes about 2 cups

1 small red onion

1 small yellow onion

1 small white onion

¾ cup red wine vinegar

5 plum tomatoes

Fresh or dried oregano, salt, ground cumin, and red pepper flakes to taste

The Forbidden Onion I have an old friend who, like me, comes from a Southern family that moved to the North. Southerners carry a lot of culinary baggage. In order to fit in up North, many of us tossed out some of our Southern kitchen ways, like eating onions. My friend's mother never cooked onions up North, and she told her children not to eat them. The smell of them frying in the kitchen or lingering on your breath identified you as a "country person," rather than a "sophisticated Northener." To this day, my friend does not eat onions, no matter how sweet or mild. And he prefers that you not cook them in your house when he's around.

You can't have a Sunday supper without greens. But a pot of fresh greens is among the most labor-intensive dishes to fix. You have to deal with each leaf of green personally. This recipe calls for a mix of greens-collards, kale, beet greens, mustard greens-the choice is yours. Cook the hardier types like collards for a while before adding more tender ones such as beet tops or turnip greens.

Pot of Greens

4 pounds mixed greens

2 yellow onions

2 cloves garlic

3 tablespoons peanut oil

About 4 cups chicken stock, or to cover

Pepper vinegar

Trim away any tough stems, then wash the greens: Rinse each leaf separately. Put all of them in a sinkful of water and let sit for a while. Now, lift them out of the sink and drain away the water and all the grit that has settled to the bottom. Repeat the sink bath until you don't see any grit when you remove the leaves. It may seem like a tedious process, but clean greens are a must. Some folks do go overboard. I won't say in which state they reside, but there are cooks who put their greens in a washing machine with detergent.

Chop the onions, and crush the garlic cloves.

In a heavy pot large enough to hold all the greens, warm the oil over medium heat. Set aside about half of the onions and add the remainder along with the garlic to the pot. Saute until softened, about 5 minutes. Add the greens, turn to coat in the oil, and then pour in the stock to cover. Bring to a boil and season with salt and pepper. Reduce the heat to low, cover, and cook until the greens are tender. The timing will depend on what you are cooking; collards can take up to 40 minutes or so, while beet greens will cook in half that time.

Transfer to a serving bowl. Pass the reserved onion and the pepper vinegar at the table for sprinkling over the top.

Serves 6

Pepper Vinegar One of the most common condiments on the Southern table is pepper vinegar, a sizzling blend of distilled white vinegar and tiny hot chili peppers. In the South, cooks put up their own supply by packing the peppers into sterilized jars, filling them up with vinegar, and adding a touch of sugar and salt. The resulting brew is delicious on greens- or anything that needs a spark.

A surprisingly good blend of taste and texture, this dish is a fine accompaniment to Oven-fried Lemon Chicken Wings (page 90). Be careful not to grind the peanuts too long, or you'll release their oils and end up with peanut butter.

Spinach & Goobers

Discard any tough stems from the spinach, then wash the greens thoroughly in a sinkful of cold water to remove every bit of grit. Shake off the excess water and chop coarsely. Thinly slice the onion and chop the garlic. In a blender or a food processor fitted with the metal blade, coarsely grind the peanuts.

In a saucepan over medium heat, warm 2 tablespoons of the olive oil. Add the onion and saute until beginning to soften, about 3 minutes. Add the spinach and continue to cook, stirring occasionally, until the spinach has wilted, about 5 minutes.

Sprinkle in the garlic and peanuts and stir to combine. Add a few tablespoons of water if the mixture seems too dry. Cover, reduce the heat to medium-low, and cook for 10 minutes, checking at the halfway point to be sure the mixture is not sticking.

Uncover, add the remaining 1 tablespoon oil, and season with salt, pepper, and nutmeg. Continue to cook, uncovered, over medium heat for 3 minutes to blend the flavors.

Taste and adjust the seasonings, then spoon into a serving bowl. Serve hot.

Serves 4

- 2 pounds spinach
- 1 small yellow onion
- 1 clove garlic
- ½ cup roasted peanuts
- 3 tablespoons olive oil
- 3 tablespoons or so water, if needed

  Salt and ground black pepper to taste

  Dash of ground nutmeg

This recipe is similar to Pot of Greens (page 122), but here three different greens are cooked together. The addition of a whole chili pepper adds a pleasant flash of heat to the mix.

Secret Garden Mixed Greens

1 bunch collard greens

1 bunch turnip greens

1 bunch mustard greens

1 yellow onion

3 cloves garlic

2 tablespoons vegetable oil

Beef or chicken stock, to cover

Salt and ground black pepper to taste

1 fresh green chili pepper

Trim away any tough stems from the greens, then wash the leaves carefully in several changes of water as directed in Pot of Greens. Chop the onion and the garlic.

In a heavy pot large enough to hold all the greens, warm the oil over medium heat. Add the onion and garlic and saute until softened, about 5 minutes. Add the greens, turn to coat in the oil, and then pour in the stock to cover. Bring to a boil and season with salt and pepper. Place the chili pepper on top. Reduce the heat to low, cover, and cook until the greens are tender, about 45 minutes, or longer depending on the age and hardiness of the greens.

Remove the chili pepper, transfer greens to a serving dish and serve.

Serves 6

Secret Gardens Some plantation owners allowed slaves to plant gardens of their own, but most masters preferred that they eat communally. The desire to "cook for we self" was too strong, however, and many slaves tended what have become known as secret gardens, where they grew vegetables to supplement their rations of "a pint of salt and a peck of corn." Even after working in the fields from sun up to sun down, or as Gullah people say, "from day clean till the sun red for down," slaves would gather food from their gardens and cook into the night.

Here, okra is given a South American accent with the additions of cilantro and dendê oil, the latter the red-orange palm oil widely used in Brazilian cooking.

Brazilian Okra with Cilantro

Trim the okra stems, but be careful not to cut into the pods. Thinly slice the onion, and mince the garlic. Chop the cilantro and measure out 3 tablespoons.

In a heavy skillet over medium heat, warm the vegetable oil. Add the okra and saute, stirring often, until tender, about 10 minutes.

Meanwhile, in a separate heavy skillet over medium heat, warm the *dende oil* . Add the onion and garlic and saute just until they begin to soften, a few minutes. When the okra is ready, add it to this skillet and season with salt and pepper. Stir over medium heat for a minute or two to blend the flavors.

Add the cilantro and mix gently. Transfer to a serving bowl and serve at once.

Serves 4 to 6

1 pound small, young okra

1 yellow onion

2 cloves garlic

Handful of fresh cilantro sprigs

1 teaspoon vegetable oil

3 tablespoons *dendê oil* (see page 24)

Salt and ground black pepper to taste

About Cilantro This pungent plant, a member of the carrot family, has worked its way into kitchens all over the United States. It is variously known as cilantro, Chinese parsley, or coriander, and is a pantry staple—both the fresh herb and the dried seeds—in Spanish, Portuguese, Chinese, East Indian, North African, and Middle Eastern kitchens. The seeds were carried to Latin America by the Spanish explorers, and were quickly adopted by the indigenous people they met up with in the New World. It is believed that the Mexicans introduced the seeds to the Native Americans living in what is now the American Southwest, and today cilantro continues to be widely cultivated by the Zunis.

You will find variations on this dish of tomatoes and okra from the Carolinas to the Caribbean. Sometimes corn, freshly cut from the cob, and/or green beans are included in the mix.

An American Ratatouille

1 small green bell pepper

1 small yellow onion

3 celery stalks

2 large tomatoes

1 pound okra

¼ cup vegetable oil

Chicken stock, if needed

Salt, ground black pepper, cayenne pepper, and dried thyme to taste

Seed the bell pepper and chop the bell pepper, onion, and celery. Peel and chop the tomatoes. Cut the okra into ½-inch-thick rounds.

In a heavy skillet over medium heat, warm the vegetable oil. Add the bell pepper, onion, and celery and saute until they begin to soften, about 5 minutes. Add the tomatoes and okra and stir well. If the mixture seems a little dry, add some chicken stock to moisten. Season with salt, black and cayenne peppers, and thyme and cook, stirring occasionally, until all the vegetables are tender and the mixture has thickened, about 15 minutes.

Spoon into a serving bowl and serve hot or at room temperature.

Serves 6, or fewer if serious okra eaters are at the table

Harvesting Okra Unlike most vegetables, okra should never be allowed to ripen before it is harvested. Left on the plant more than ten weeks, the pods become tough, fibrous, and hard on the diner's digestion. This fast-growing vegetable has never experienced great popularity in the United States outside the South. Indeed, in some national surveys it has ranked high on the list of least favorite vegetables by adults and children alike. I can only surmise they were all fed pods that were left too long in the garden. A mean-spirited okra basher made up a blasphemous proverb—God don't eat okra!

This is one of the great culinary marriages – okra and cornmeal cooked together. The serving bowl is buttered so that the fungi won't stick to it.

Caribbean Fungi

About ½ pound okra

Butter for greasing bowl

4 cups water

1 cup coarse yellow cornmeal

Salt to taste

Cut the okra into ¼-inch-thick rounds; you should have 2 cups. Grease a serving bowl liberally with butter.

Pour the water into a large saucepan and bring to a boil over high heat. Slowly add the cornmeal while stirring constantly with a wooden spoon.

Then add the okra, again stirring constantly. Season with salt, reduce the heat to low, and cook, stirring constantly, until the cornmeal is creamy, 20 to 25 minutes.

Remove from the heat and pour into the buttered bowl. Serve immediately.

Serves 6

Cornmeal Dishes On the Virgin Islands, the pairing of cornmeal and okra is called fungi, and on Barbados coucou. Indeed, this dish is a staple throughout the Caribbean under a variety of names. Fungi is labor-intensive. You have to be constantly stirring, and a wooden spoon is always used. I have a friend whose most prized culinary treasure is her grandmother's fungi spoon. In parts of the South, the cornmeal without the okra-a cornmeal mush-is called cush-cush (or couche-couche) and sometimes has a little sugar added it. I like it with something "wet" spooned over it, such as Low Country Boiled Fish (page 65).

Brazilian cooks use kale for this dish, but I have found that much of the kale available in the United States cooks too soft, so I prefer collards. The success of the dish depends on very finely shredding the greens.

Brazilian Couve

Discard any tough stems, then wash the greens thoroughly in a sinkful of cold water to remove every bit of grit. Shake off the excess water. Working in batches, fold the greens into envelope shapes, then slice very, very thinly.

Bring a large pot of water to a boil. Plunge the greens into the water and boil for 1 minute. Drain well, then plunge them into cold water. Drain well again.

In a large, heavy skillet over medium heat, warm the oil. Add the shredded greens and saute until very tender, about 10 minutes. Season with salt and black and cayenne peppers. Spoon into a serving bowl and serve hot.

Serves 4

2 pounds kale or collard greens

¼ cup vegetable oil

Salt, ground black pepper, and cayenne pepper to taste

Feijoada In Brazil, couve is a classic accompaniment to the national dish, feijoada, a preparation that many food historians believe has an African origin. Feijoada combines black beans and assorted meats – sausages, beef tongue, pig's ears and feet, fresh and cured pork – and is richly flavored with onions, garlic, and chilies. A palm heart salad, white rice, orange slices, and farofa de manteiga (ground manioc, also known as cassava, toasted in a skillet with butter) are also always part of the spread. Cachaça, a volcanic white rum distilled from sugarcane, traditionally accompanies the feast.

When it comes to succotash, fresh is always best: baby lima beans right out of their pods and corn cut from the cob. If frozen vegetables are all you have, make it anyway. It just won't taste as good.

Real Southern Succotash

3 thick slices bacon

1 cup water, or as needed

2 cups baby lima beans (about 1½ pounds)

2 cups corn kernels (from 3 to 4 ears)

1 cup okra

Salt and ground black pepper to taste

Dash of cayenne pepper

In a heavy saucepan over medium-high heat, cook the bacon until crisp and the fat is rendered, 3 to 5 minutes. Transfer to paper towels to drain. Add 1 cup water to the bacon fat remaining in the pan and bring to a boil over high heat, scraping up any burned-on bits. Add the lima beans, cover, reduce the heat to low, and cook until nearly tender, about 20 minutes.

Cut or crumble the bacon into pieces. Add the bacon, corn, okra, salt, and black and cayenne peppers to the limas. Raise the heat to medium and cook until the okra is tender, about 10 minutes, adding more water to the pan if the mixture begins to dry out.

Taste and adjust the seasonings, then serve.

Serves 6

Succotash Riffs Succotash is derived from a Native American word that means stew, and that gives license to have almost anything happen in the pot. Some people like the limas and corn creamed. Some cook them with ham. Still others use flour to bind it all together. And since succotash is really a stew, a variety of vegetables can be tossed in along with the basics. I like to sometimes add a couple of ripe, red tomatoes.

The name of this dish translates to Moors and Christians. Made with black beans and white rice, it is a hearty component of the Cuban menu. Fried eggs and fried plantains sometimes join it on the plate.

Moros y Cristianos

1 cup dried black beans

1 small green bell pepper

1 yellow onion

2 cloves garlic

¼ cup olive oil

Ground black pepper, cayenne pepper, and ground cumin to taste

4 ½ cups water

Salt to taste

2 cups long-grain white rice

Pick over the black beans, discarding any misshapen peas or grit and rinse in cold water. Place in a large bowl with water to cover generously. Let soak overnight.

The next day, seed the bell pepper and chop the bell pepper, onion, and garlic. Drain the beans.

In a large saucepan over medium heat, warm half of the olive oil. Add the bell pepper, onion, and garlic and saute until softened, about 5 minutes. Add the drained beans, black and cayenne peppers, cumin, and water and bring to a boil. Reduce the heat to low and cook, uncovered, until the beans are nearly tender, about 1½ hours. Season with salt.

Add the rice, stir well, cover, and continue to cook until the rice and beans are tender, about 20 minutes longer. If the liquid has cooked away before the rice is done, add a little more water. Taste and adjust the seasonings. Remove from the heat, stir in the remaining oil, and let rest, covered, for about 10 minutes before serving.

Serves 6 to 8

Caribbean Beans The Cubans are divided on beans. Black beans are eaten in the west, around Havana, while those living on the eastern part of the island prefer a dish of red beans and rice, probably due to the influence of nearby Jamaica and Haiti, where red beans are popular. Red beans are also regularly paired with rice in Guadalupe, are the base of a soup with dumplings on St. Croix, and are simmered in a stew with pork and sausages in the Dominican Republic.

Red kidney beans are traditionally used for this recipe in New Orleans, but pinto, Great Northerns, or even a bag of mixed beans would be tasty. You can use a ham bone or another kind of smoked meat in place of the ham hocks, or you can leave the meat out altogether and stir in a couple of tablespoons of olive oil just before serving to boost the flavor. Be sure to serve the beans over a mound of white rice. As Louis Armstrong used to say, "Red beans and ricely yours."

New Orleans Wash Day Red Beans

Pick over the red beans, discarding any misshapen peas or grit and rinse in cold water. Place in a large bowl with water to cover generously. Let soak overnight.

The next day, seed the bell pepper and chop the bell pepper, onion, celery, and garlic. Drain the beans.

In a large pot over medium heat, warm the olive oil. Add the bell pepper, onion, celery, and garlic and saute until softened, about 5 minutes. Add the ham hocks, drained beans, thyme, black and cayenne peppers, bay leaf, and water, and bring to a boil. Reduce the heat to low and cook uncovered, stirring often, until the beans are tender, about 1½ hours.

Transfer the beans and ham hocks to a large serving bowl and serve hot. The flavors are even better if the beans are cooled and then reheated the next day.

Serves 6

2¼ cups (1 pound) dried red beans

1 small green bell pepper

1 small yellow onion

1 celery stalk

2 cloves garlic

2 tablespoons olive oil

1 to 2 pounds ham hocks, cut into 2-inch rounds

Dried thyme, ground black pepper, and cayenne pepper to taste

1 bay leaf

4 quarts water

Wash Day Meals In another time, when everything was done according to tradition, Monday was always wash day. That meant cooking something that didn't require too much watching. A pot of beans was the answer, and in New Orleans that pot always held a batch of simmering red beans. That's how wash day beans got its name. Even with the advent of automatic washers, a pot of beans is still the answer to a busy schedule and a discriminating palate.

For Geechee/Gullah people, proper rice is "dry and every grain to itself." Failure results in your name being scandalized, and eye contact forever avoided. And of course, no one will ever come to your house to eat, nor will they eat your rice at a potluck. The rule to achieve the perfect result is simple. You can multiply out this formula to feed whatever number of people show up at your table.

Proper Geechee Rice

1 part long-grain white rice

2 parts water

Rinse the rice until the water runs clear (or as Grandma Sula used to say, "rinse it three times, and then once more").

In a heavy saucepan over high heat, combine the rice and water and cover with the lid ajar.

Bring the water to a boil, shift the lid so that it covers the pan tightly, turn down the heat to very low, and cook for 20 minutes until the rice is tender and the liquid is absorbed. Never, never, never stir the rice during this time. Don't even think about uncovering the pot to peek.

Remove from the heat and let rest for 10 minutes before serving. Your rice will be proper.

My First Proper Rice I don't remember exactly how old I was the first time I cooked a pot of "proper rice." But I remember exactly the way I felt when my Grandmama Sula asked my mother, "Now, who cooked this rice?" "She did," said Mama. "Well," said Grandmama Sula, "it sure is cooked proper." I thought my chest would burst with pride.

When I can get real tomatoes — ripe, red, full of flavor — I always use them for this dish. But too often the tomatoes in the market are tasteless, so I resort to canned crushed tomatoes. If you can find good fresh ones, use them. The rice is delicious with hot Skillet Corn Bread (see page 148).

Low Country Red Rice

Chop the onion. Have the can of tomatoes opened and ready to use.

In a heavy saucepan over medium-high heat, fry the bacon until crisp and the fat is rendered, 3 to 5 minutes. Transfer to paper towels to drain. Pour off all but 2 tablespoons of the bacon fat from the pan.

Return the pan to medium heat and add the onion. Saute until it begins to soften, about 2 minutes. Add the rice and saute until the grains are coated with the bacon fat and are very hot, about 5 minutes. Add the tomatoes, salt, and black and cayenne peppers, mixing well. Pour in the stock or water and bring to a boil. Cover tightly, reduce the heat to low, and cook until the rice is tender and the liquid is absorbed, about 30 minutes. Do not stir the rice during this time.

Spoon the rice into a serving bowl and crumble the bacon over the top. Serve at once.

Serves 4 to 6

1 small yellow onion

1 can (14 ounces) crushed tomatoes

3 thick slices bacon

1 cup long-grain white rice

Salt, ground black pepper, and cayenne pepper to taste

1 cup chicken stock or water

Charleston Red Rice Some folks call this dish Charleston red rice, but it's eaten up and down and around the Carolinas and Georgia, so I call it Low Country Red Rice. My cousin Skeet says, "Charleston people will 'tief' anything. They even stole the dance from neighboring James Island, so it comes as no surprise that they have tried "to tief the red rice from the rest of the Low Country." Everyone has his or her own way of making real red rice, so don't write, call, or e-mail me that this is not real red rice.

This recipe is adapted from one created by Dr. Carver. The original called for cooking in the oven for 3 hours, which I found to be much too long. I have shortened the time to 45 minutes or so, baking it much as you would a rice pudding. It is wonderful for serving with roasted or grilled poultry or meats.

Dr. George Washington Carver's Peanuts Baked with Rice

⅓ cup long-grain white rice

About ¾ cup roasted peanuts

½ teaspoon salt

⅓ cup sugar

4 cups milk

Preheat an oven to 350 degrees F. Grease a 9-by-13-inch baking dish with butter.

Rinse the rice in cold running water and drain well. In a blender or a food processor fitted with the metal blade, coarsely grind the peanuts; you will need 1 cup coarsely ground. In a cup or small dish, stir together the salt and sugar.

Scatter a little rice evenly over the bottom of the prepared dish, and top with a scattering of the peanuts. Sprinkle on some of the sugar mixture. Repeat layers until the ingredients are used up, ending with a layer of peanuts. Pour the milk into the dish.

Bake until the rice is tender and the liquid is absorbed, 45 minutes to 1 hour. Serve hot directly from the dish.

Serves 6

The Peanut's Long Journey Peanuts have been growing in South America for over three thousand years. They were "discovered" by the Spanish and Portuguese explorers in the sixteenth century and carried with them to Africa, where they were quickly cultivated. Then the slave trade carried the peanuts back across the water to Southern plantations, where at first they were considered suitable only for feeding livestock and the poor. But many slave families planted them in their garden plots and were soon roasting them in the hearth of the big-house kitchen, where they were introduced to the plantation master and his family. The brilliant agricultural chemist, research scientist, and educator, Dr. George Washington Carver, suggested growing peanuts to replace the cotton economy and to help feed the people. His work resulted in more than 300 uses for this new crop, which included not only food applications but also everything from paints, dyes, and shoe polish to a massage oil to help polio victims.

In the 1960s, when I lived on Manhattan's Lower East Side, one of my favorite places to eat was a small joint that served grits and just about anything you can name — grits 'n' salmon croquettes, grits 'n' eggs, grits 'n' stewed shrimp, grits 'n' gravy, grits 'n' sausage, grits 'n' grillades. Grits are wonderfully versatile because they are bland and take on the flavor of whatever is served with them.

True Grits

1 cup stone-ground regular grits

4 cups water

Salt to taste

Place the grits in a large bowl, add water to cover generously. Using a wire skimmer, remove any chaff that rises to the surface. Drain well.

In a saucepan, combine the water, grits, and salt and bring to a boil. Reduce the heat to low and cook, stirring constantly, until the grits have a flowing consistency, about 30 minutes. They should be neither too soft nor too stiff.

Transfer to a serving dish and serve piping hot.

Serves 4

About Grits Grits are dried kernels of field corn (hominy) that have been hulled and then coarsely cracked. They come in regular, quick-cooking, and instant forms, although I advise avoiding the instant, as the texture and taste are disappointing. Quick-cooking grits are passable, but they will taste better if you leave them on the stove a little longer than the 5 minutes the box generally indicates. Stone-ground regular grits have the best flavor and cook in about 30 to 40 minutes. In the past, folks always rinsed the grits before cooking; today that step is unnecessary. Despite that, I still put stone-ground grits in a large bowl, add water to cover, and then skim off the chaff that floats to the top before cooking them. Most package directions say to add grits to boiling water, but I start mine in cold. You don't have to be a Southerner to eat grits, but only a Southerner would write:

> *True grits*
> *More grits*
> *Fish, grits and collards*
> *Life is good where grits are swallered.*
> *— Roy Blount, Jr.*

There is no use in making these dumplings unless you plan to cook up a Pot of Greens (page 122). Tender, young turnip greens beg for these dumplings, but any flavorful greens will do.

Cornmeal Dumplings

In a bowl, using a wooden spoon, stir together the cornmeal, flour, baking powder, and salt. Add the corn oil, mix well, and then add enough milk to form a thick but not stiff batter.

Drop the cornmeal mixture by teaspoonfuls onto the surface of the greens about 20 minutes before the greens are ready. Cover and don't touch the lid for 20 minutes. They'll be done in that amount of time.

Ladle the dumplings and greens into a bowl. Sprinkle with some freshly ground black pepper and some hot sauce, if you like, and enjoy some earthy eating.

Makes enough dumplings for one recipe Pot of Greens (page 122).

1 cup yellow cornmeal

3 tablespoons all-purpose flour

2 teaspoons baking powder

1 teaspoon salt

¼ cup corn oil

About 3 tablespoons milk

Freshly ground black pepper

Favorite hot-pepper sauce (optional)

This is like a pan of macaroni and cheese. It travels well to church suppers and potlucks. It is easy to assemble, but its success depends on a good oven with steady, even heat.

Corn Pudding

Butter

3 or 4 ears of corn

¼ cup butter

2 eggs

1 cup evaporated milk

1 ½ teaspoons sugar

Salt and coarsely ground black pepper to taste

½ teaspoon baking powder

Preheat an oven to 350 degrees F. Grease an 8-inch square pan with some butter.

Cut the kernels, along with all their milky pulp, from the ears of corn (see sidebar) and measure out 2 cups. Melt the ¼ cup butter.

In a large bowl, beat the eggs until well blended. Add the corn kernels, milk, sugar, and salt and pepper and mix well. Add the baking powder and again mix well.

Pour the corn mixture into the prepared dish and drizzle the melted butter evenly over the top. Bake until set, about 30 minutes. Serve hot or at room temperature.

Serves 6

Removing Corn Kernels If you love corn puddings, corn chowders, and all other such corn dishes, you might want to buy a little tool called a corn kernel remover. It can be adjusted to remove just the kernels neatly, or when you want a creamier batch of corn, to extract the "milk" as well. You can also remove them the old-fashioned way: Shuck the ears of corn and remove all the silk. Then, with a sharp knife, cut off three or four rows of kernels with each trip of the knife blade from the top to the bottom of the cob. Don't cut too deeply if you want only the kernels. If you want the milky pulp, too, once you have cut away the kernels, stand the ear stem end down in a shallow bowl and run the back of the knife down the cob to force out the pulp.

The name of this fluffy pudding comes from Pompano Beach, Florida, and the idea for it originated with the Florida Sweet Corn Exchange. Unlike the previous recipe, this one can't travel anywhere, except from the oven to the table. You must serve it immediately or it will lose its loft.

Corn Pudding Pompano

Preheat an oven to 350 degrees F. Grease a 9-by-13-inch baking dish with 1 tablespoon of the butter.

Cut the kernels, along with all their milky pulp, from the ears of corn (see sidebar, page 140) and measure out 2 cups. Melt the remaining butter.

Separate the eggs, placing the whites in a medium bowl. Using an electric mixer, beat the egg whites until stiff peaks form. Place the egg yolks in a large bowl and beat until blended. Add the corn, milk, salt, pepper, and sugar to the egg yolks and mix well. Fold in the beaten whites.

Pour the corn mixture into the prepared dish. Bake until set, about 30 minutes. Serve immediately.

Serves 6

3 tablespoons butter

10 ears of corn

4 eggs

2 cups milk

1½ teaspoons salt

Dash of ground black pepper

2 tablespoons sugar

Fried catfish without hush puppies is like pancakes without syrup.

Hush Puppies

2 cups yellow cornmeal

1 teaspoon baking soda

1 teaspoon baking powder

1 teaspoon salt

2 tablespoons vegetable shortening

2 eggs

2 scallions (optional)

1 cup milk or buttermilk, or as needed

Vegetable oil for frying

In a medium bowl, stir together the cornmeal, baking soda, baking powder, and salt.

In a small pan, place the shortening over low heat just until melted. In a small bowl, beat the eggs until blended. If using the scallions, chop them, including the tender green tops.

Add the 1 cup milk or buttermilk, shortening, eggs, and the scallions, if using, to the cornmeal mixture and stir until well mixed. The mixture should have the consistency of a thick batter. If it is too stiff, add a little more milk or buttermilk.

Pour the oil into a heavy saucepan or deep skillet to a depth of about 2 inches. Place over medium-high heat until the oil is hot but not smoking. Working in batches, carefully drop the batter into the hot oil by heaping rounded spoonfuls, forming balls about 1½ inches in diameter. Fry, turning as necessary to brown evenly, until light golden brown, 2 to 3 minutes. Using a slotted utensil, transfer to paper towels to drain.

Serve piping hot, fresh out of the pan.

Serves 4

A Dog Story According to legend, hush puppies got their name when some fishermen were down by the riverside cooking their catch. They dredged their catfish in cornmeal before dropping it into the hot fat. The smell of the frying fish was so tantalizing that dogs from all around started yelping for handouts. The fishermen, not wanting to give up their supper, formed balls of cornmeal, dropped them into the hot fat, scooped them out, and then fed them to the dogs, while saying "hush, puppy."

Breads

I have found that sometimes people want more than one corn muffin, but 2 muffins are too many. So I often use pans with miniature muffin cups. That way diners can eat 4 or 5 muffins without any problem. For a yummy variation, add ½ cup white corn kernels to the batter with the chilies.

White Corn Muffins with Green Chilies

2 cups white cornmeal

1 tablespoon baking powder

1 teaspoon salt

½ teaspoon baking soda

2 eggs

1 cup milk

¼ cup corn oil

½ cup well-drained canned chopped green chilies

Preheat an oven to 450 degrees F. Liberally grease a standard 12-cup muffin tin.

In a medium bowl, stir together the cornmeal, baking powder, salt, and baking soda. In a large bowl, beat the eggs until blended, then stir in the milk, corn oil, and chilies. Add the cornmeal mixture and stir just until there are no lumps; do not overmix.

Pour the batter into the prepared muffin tin, dividing it evenly among the cups and filling each cup about two-thirds full. Bake until risen and golden on top, 15 to 20 minutes.

Remove from the oven and let cool for a few minutes before turning the muffins out of the tin. If necessary, ease them out with the tip of a sharp knife.

Makes 12 muffins

Roman Holiday On my first trip to Europe, I was trying to separate myself from such Geechee food as cornbread and couche couche and enter the world of cosmopolitan dining. In restaurants I would order only what I believed to be the most sophisticated dishes. Most of the time I couldn't even pronounce the names— and often didn't even like the dish. But I was determined to "educate" my palate. Then one balmy night in Rome, I was out with some locals who insisted on ordering dinner for all of us at their favorite restaurant. As we say in the Low Country, I shut my mouth wide open with surprise when the centerpiece of the meal arrived. They called it polenta, but I knew it looked like Southern grits, cornmeal mush or couche couche. That night I took a giant step in what has become an ongoing culinary journey that so often leads me home.

The secret to making sure your cornbread has a crisp crust is to preheat the cast-iron skillet until very hot before you add the batter. You can also put this batter in a standard muffin tin, in which case you will end up with a dozen muffins. Remember to preheat the muffin tin, too. If you buy a cornbread mix instead, be sure to get one without the sugar. Remember, it's cornbread, not corn cake.

Skillet Cornbread

2 cups stone-ground cornmeal, preferably white

1 teaspoon baking soda

1 teaspoon salt

1 teaspoon baking powder

1 egg

1 cup buttermilk

Preheat an oven to 450 degrees F. Lightly grease a 9-inch cast-iron skillet with butter and place it in the oven while it preheats. It should take about 10 minutes.

In a medium bowl, stir together the cornmeal, baking soda, salt, and baking powder. In a large bowl, beat the egg until blended, then stir in the buttermilk. Add the cornmeal mixture and stir just until there are no lumps; do not overmix.

Remove the preheated skillet from the oven and pour the batter into it. The batter should sizzle as it hits the hot pan. (If it doesn't, your pan wasn't hot enough; remember to preheat it fully next time.) Slip the skillet back into the oven and bake until the top is golden brown and crusty, about 25 minutes. Serve hot from the skillet.

Makes one 9-inch round loaf; serves 4 to 6

Cornmeal Colors White, yellow or blue cornmeal—it's a matter of personal preference as to which one you use. Some people prefer to fry fish in yellow cornmeal because they claim it browns faster. I like white cornmeal for making cornbread because I like the way it looks: pale with a beautiful brown top. Some cooks don't like blue cornmeal simply because it is dark and looks different. But I think the corn taste stays pretty much the same no matter what the color.

My daughter Chandra has lived in Albuquerque for a number of years. There are two outstanding things about that: I have learned to spell Albuquerque, and I have learned to appreciate blue cornmeal.

Albuquerque Blue Corn Bread

Preheat an oven to 450 degrees F. Lightly grease a 9-inch cast-iron skillet with butter and place it in the oven while it preheats. It should take about 10 minutes.

In a medium bowl, stir together the cornmeal, flour, baking powder, baking soda, and salt. In a large bowl, beat the egg until blended, then stir in the corn oil and buttermilk. Add the cornmeal mixture and stir just until there are no lumps; do not overmix.

Remove the preheated skillet from the oven and pour the batter into it. The batter should sizzle as it hits the hot pan. (If it doesn't, your pan wasn't hot enough; remember to preheat it fully next time.)

Slip the skillet back into the oven and bake until the top is golden brown and crusty, about 25 minutes. It will rise slightly higher in the center, but don't let that worry you. Serve hot from the skillet.

Makes one 9-inch round loaf; serves 4 to 6

1⅓ cups blue cornmeal

⅔ cup unbleached all-purpose flour

1 teaspoon baking powder

1 teaspoon baking soda

1 teaspoon salt

1 egg

½ cup corn oil

1⅓ cups buttermilk

The "peanut" in this bread is peanut butter and peanut oil. In Africa and Indonesia, plenty of peanut butter is made, but not for putting in bread recipes, or even for smearing on bread. Cooks there use one of America's favorite sandwich spreads for thickening and flavoring soups and sauces.

Carrot & Peanut Bread

Preheat an oven to 350 degrees F. Grease a 9-by-5-inch loaf pan with butter.

Peel the carrots and finely grate them into a bowl; measure out 2 cups.

In a large bowl, combine the sugar, peanut butter, and peanut oil. Beat together until creamy. Add the eggs, mixing well. Stir in the grated carrots and the vanilla.

In a medium bowl, stir together the flour, baking soda, baking powder, nutmeg, and allspice. Divide the flour mixture into 3 batches. Beat the flour mixture into the carrot mixture alternately with the milk, beginning and ending with the flour mixture.

Transfer the batter to the prepared pan. Bake until a cake tester inserted into the center comes out clean, about 1 hour. Remove from the oven and place on a wire rack to cool. Then turn out of the pan and serve.

Makes 1 loaf

3 or 4 large carrots

1 cup firmly packed brown sugar

¾ cup unsalted smooth peanut butter

½ cup peanut oil

2 eggs

1 teaspoon vanilla extract

1¾ cups all-purpose flour

1 teaspoon baking soda

1 teaspoon baking powder

½ teaspoon ground nutmeg

½ teaspoon ground allspice

½ cup milk

A Few Peanut Statistics Half of the peanuts consumed in the United States are eaten in peanut butter — about 800 million pounds a year. According to the Peanut Advisory Board, that's enough to coat the entire Grand Canyon — depending, of course, on how thick you like to spread it. Peanut butter is about 50 percent fat, 29 percent protein, and 17 percent carbohydrate. Fortunately, the fat is mostly the unsaturated kind, which actually helps to lower cholesterol levels in the blood.

Everybody, at one point or another, faces the same problem: what to do with old, soft bananas. The solution? Make this bread. If you aren't worried about the extra calories, add your favorite nuts—pecans, walnuts, or peanuts.

Ripe Banana Bread

4 ripe bananas

1 cup nuts of choice (optional)

⅓ cup butter, at room temperature

½ cup sugar

2 eggs

1 teaspoon lemon extract

2 cups all-purpose flour

2 teaspoons baking powder

½ teaspoon ground nutmeg

½ teaspoon ground cinnamon

½ teaspoon ground allspice

Pinch of salt

Preheat an oven to 350 degrees F. Grease a 9-by-5-inch loaf pan with some of the butter.

Peel the bananas and place in a bowl. Mash with a fork, ridding them of all lumps. Chop the nuts, if using.

In a large bowl, combine the butter and sugar. Using a wooden spoon, beat together until creamy. Add the eggs, mixing well. Stir in the mashed bananas and the lemon extract.

In a medium bowl, stir together the flour, baking powder, nutmeg, cinnamon, allspice, and salt. Gradually add the flour mixture to the butter mixture, blending well. If the mixture seems a little dry, stir in a few tablespoons water. Stir in the nuts, if using.

Transfer the batter to the prepared pan. Bake until a cake tester inserted into the center comes out clean, about 1 hour and 10 minutes. Remove from the oven and place on a wire rack to cool. Then turn out of the pan and serve.

Makes 1 loaf

The ubiquitous Banana It should come as no surprise that outside of banana-growing country—the tropical and subtropical world—the United States is home to the planet's leading banana consumers. We slice them atop our morning cereal, bake them into bread, blend them into health drinks, fold them into cream pies, and just eat them out of hand. We assured ourselves a steady supply of these favorite fruits by establishing the international banana trade. Although the commercial interest in bananas began in the mid-1880s, with the founding of the Boston Fruit Company, it was not until after World War I and the invention of refrigerated boats that bananas traveled the world. Of course, Caribbean cooks, who have always been able to pick bananas right from the trees, have long been renowned for flambeing them with rum, frying them into fritters, and baking them into custards.

There is nothing like the smell of homemade bread baking. This quick-and-easy Caribbean-inspired loaf has a divine aroma and a down-to-earth flavor that makes it hard to resist eating it straight from the oven.

Breads **153**

Coconut Bread

Preheat an oven to 350 degrees F. Grease a 9-by-5-inch loaf pan with butter. Sift together the flour, baking powder, and salt into a large bowl. In a small bowl, beat the egg until blended. Place the shortening in a small pan over medium heat just until melted. Remove from the heat and let cool.

To the flour mixture, add the beaten egg, cooled shortening, milk, and sugar and stir to mix thoroughly. Stir in the vanilla and coconut until blended. The dough will be soft and quite malleable.

Lightly flour a work surface. Turn out the dough onto it and knead it with a few quick strokes. Form into a loaf shape and place in the prepared pan.

Bake until golden brown and a cake tester inserted into the center comes out clean, 45 to 50 minutes.

Makes 1 loaf

2 cups all-purpose flour

1 teaspoon baking powder

Dash of salt

1 egg

¼ cup vegetable shortening

¼ cup milk

½ cup sugar

1 teaspoon vanilla extract

1 cup grated dried coconut

About Coconuts The meat and milk of the coconut are used in dishes and drinks on all the Caribbean islands. If you want to be authentic, here's how to crack a coconut: using an ice pick or the tip of a sharp knife, pierce two of the three black spots, or "eyes," near the top of the coconut. Drain out the liquid; this is called coconut water and it's a refreshing drink. Now, place the coconut on a sturdy surface — a sidewalk might be best — and strike it with a hammer until it breaks up into manageably sized pieces. Using a sharp paring knife, pry the white meat from the shell, then peel off the brown skin. (Sometimes getting the meat out is difficult; try putting the coconut pieces in a warm oven for about 15 minutes to loosen it.) Grate the meat and use as desired in recipes. If making coconut milk, grate the meat as fine as possible, place in a bowl, and pour over a cup of boiling water for each cup of grated meat. Let stand for an hour, then squeeze through a kitchen towel to extract the rich milk.

These are a variation on the South's classic baking-powder biscuits. Spread with fresh butter – no margarine please – and watermelon rind preserves. Or serve with honey and butter alongside some stone-ground hominy grits and salmon croquettes for breakfast.

Sweet Potato Biscuits

1 large or 2 medium-sized sweet potatoes

1¼ cups all-purpose flour

1 tablespoon baking powder

½ teaspoon salt

3 tablespoons vegetable shortening

About ½ cup milk

Scrub the sweet potatoes but do not peel. Bring a large saucepan of water to a boil. Add the sweet potatoes and boil until tender when pierced with a fork, 30 to 40 minutes; the timing will depend on the size of the sweet potatoes. Drain well, let cool, and peel. Place the sweet potatoes in a bowl and mash with a potato masher until no lumps remain. Measure out 1 cup; reserve the remainder for another use.

Preheat an oven to 450 degrees F. Grease a baking sheet with butter.

Sift together the flour, baking powder, and salt into a large bowl. Add the shortening and, using a pastry blender or 2 knives, cut in the shortening until the mixture resembles coarse meal. Add the cold mashed sweet potatoes and stir to mix well. Add ¼ cup of the milk and stir to form a soft, workable dough. If the dough is too stiff, add a little additional milk.

Lightly flour a work surface. Turn out the dough onto it and knead it with a few quick strokes. Using a rolling pin, roll out the dough ½ inch thick. Using a 2-inch biscuit cutter, cut out as many biscuits as possible and arrange on the prepared baking sheet. Gather together any scraps, reroll, and cut out more biscuits. You should have 18 biscuits in all.

Bake until golden brown, 12 to 15 minutes. Remove from the oven and serve hot or warm. Makes eighteen 2-inch biscuits

Southern Biscuits In the Low Country, as in the rest of the South, biscuits are a staple. Traditionally, in homes and in restaurants, cooks turned out panfuls of them. The most skilled mixed and rolled every batch by hand, making biscuits so light and fluffy they would melt in your mouth without a pat of butter. These days, while biscuits remain popular, most of them come to the table out of a cardboard tube rather than a mixing bowl.

Along with Cornmeal Dumplings (page 139), hoecakes are wonderful companions to simmered greens. Some hoecake recipes call for flour and shortening and other ingredients along with the cornmeal, but in my kitchen I always made them this way—the old-fashioned way. There is a saying down home, "If you wants to bake a hoecake, and wants to bake it good and done, slap it on a hoe, and turn it to the sun."

Hoecakes

Place the cornmeal and salt in a bowl and stir together to mix. Add the boiling water a little at a time, stirring constantly until you have a dough that is soft yet firm enough to shape into thin pancakelike disks 2 to 3 inches in diameter.

Place a cast-iron skillet over medium-high heat and pour in a little oil. Tilt the skillet to coat the bottom evenly. When the oil is hot, add the cakes, being careful not to crowd the pan. Cook until browned on one side, just a few minutes. Flip them and cook on the second side until browned.

Transfer to a serving plate and keep warm while you cook remaining cakes. Serve hot.

Serves 4

1 cup cornmeal

Dash of salt

About 1½ cups boiling water

Vegetable oil

This recipe comes from my Texan friend Ella Mae. She claims this is the best johnnycake recipe I'll ever find. I can't say she's lying. It's the only johnnycake recipe I've ever tested — and it's wonderful! Serve these cornmeal squares for supper in place of potatoes.

Johnnycakes

Preheat an oven to 350 degrees F. Grease an 8-inch square baking pan with vegetable shortening.

Sift together the flour, cornmeal, sugar, and baking powder into a large bowl. Place the shortening in a small pan over medium heat just until melted. Remove from the heat and let cool. Separate the eggs, placing the whites in a medium bowl. Using an electric mixer, beat the egg whites until stiff peaks form. Lightly beat the egg yolks until blended.

Add the egg yolks, milk, and melted shortening to the flour mixture, and stir to mix well. Scoop up about one-fourth of the egg whites and stir into the flour mixture. Then add the remaining whites, folding them in just until no white streaks remain; do not overmix or you will deflate the mixture.

Transfer to the prepared pan. Bake until browned and set, 20 to 25 minutes. Cut into squares and serve hot or at room temperature.

Serves 6

1 cup all-purpose flour

1 cup yellow cornmeal

½ cup sugar

2 teaspoons baking powder

3 tablespoons vegetable shortening

2 eggs

1 cup milk

The Origins Of The Johnnycake Close relatives of the hoecake (page 155) and corn pone, johnnycakes go by other names. Some folks call them journey cakes, citing the fact that they were regularly tucked into the packs of early travelers. Others call them Shawnee cakes, believing the basic recipe was passed along to the settlers by the Indians, who had long relied on corn in their diets. And then there are the controversies over how to make them: thick or thin, from white or yellow cornmeal, with regular milk or powdered milk.

Desserts & More

When folks say a recipe is so simple a child can do it, it often isn't true. But trust me. This one is that simple. My grandson, Oscar, made dozens of these on the "Americas' Family Kitchen." And the cookies are delicious.

Oscar Brown Sugar Cookies

⅔ cup vegetable shortening

½ cup firmly packed light brown sugar

1 tablespoon water

2 eggs

Dash of salt

¼ teaspoon baking soda

⅓ cup unsweetened cocoa powder

1½ cups all-purpose flour

1 teaspoon vanilla extract

2 cups semisweet chocolate chips

2 cups flaked dried coconut

Preheat an oven to 375 degrees F.

In a large bowl, combine the shortening, brown sugar, and water. Beat until well blended. Add the eggs one at a time, beating well after each addition. Then beat in the salt, baking soda, cocoa, and flour until thoroughly combined.

Stir in the vanilla and chocolate chips. Spread the coconut on a plate. Using a spoon, scoop out small lumps of the dough and shape between your palms into balls ½ inch in diameter. Then roll the balls in the coconut, coating them evenly. As the balls are coated, arrange them on an ungreased baking sheet, making sure they do not touch.

Bake until they flatten slightly, about 7 minutes. Using a spatula, transfer the cookies to another baking sheet to cool. Store layered between sheets of waxed paper in a tin with a tight-fitting top. They will keep for as long as little fingers stay out of the tin.

Makes about 36 cookies

Brown Baby One of jazz legend Oscar Brown, Jr.'s big hits in the sixties was "Brown Baby." It spoke to the hope that our children would have a better life and "walk down the freedom road." Like so many other mothers, I sang this song as a lullaby to my children. Never in my wildest dreams did I think that my grandchild would be a Brown baby. Oscar Brown IV, or Little O as he is called, is the son of Oscar Brown III, who is the son of Oscar Brown, Jr., who is the son of Oscar Brown, Big O. Oscar IV and I have a lot of fun in the kitchen. He has great curiosity and is a quick study. Oscar, his cousin Charlotte Rose, and I often go food shopping together, and I teach them the secrets of marketing, just as my father taught me. I think that it has worked. One day in the supermarket, he yelled down the produce counter, "Grandmother, the eggplants are firm."

If you have never made candy before, make your first candy this Brazilian sweet. It is easy and you will not be disappointed by the taste.

Peanut Croquettes

1 pound shelled peanuts

1 cup sugar

1 egg yolk

2 teaspoons butter

¼ cup milk

Dash of salt

Sugar for coating

Preheat an oven to 325 degrees F. Spread the peanuts on a baking sheet. Place in the oven and toast until lightly browned and fragrant, about 10 minutes. Transfer the warm nuts to a kitchen towel and rub them between the palms of your hands to remove the skins. Working in batches, grind in a nut mill or in a food processor fitted with the metal blade. Be careful when grinding the nuts, as they release their oils and can quickly turn to paste. Check every few seconds, or you may end up with peanut butter.

Butter a large platter. In a saucepan, combine the ground nuts, sugar, egg yolk, butter, milk and salt. Stir to mix, then place over medium heat. Cook, stirring constantly, until all the ingredients are fully combined and the mixture leaves the sides of the pan, about 7 minutes. Turn out the mixture onto the buttered platter and let cool.

Form a thin layer of sugar on a plate. Shape the cooled peanut mixture into small balls or ovals the size of a large marble. Roll them in the sugar. Store between sheets of waxed paper in an airtight container at room temperature for up to 1 week.

Makes about 40 candies

comfort, comfort, comfort. Some cooks add brandy or other elaborations, but this is a basic rice pudding and it's absolutely scrumptious just as it is. In fact, it's so good that when my grandson, Oscar, was only seven years old and traveling unaccompanied on a plane back home to Albuquerque, he took this pudding along for a snack.

Old Timey Rice Pudding with Golden Raisins

Preheat an oven to 350 degrees F. Grease a 9-inch square baking dish with butter.

In a saucepan, combine the water and salt and bring to a boil. Add the rice, reduce the heat to medium-low, and cook, uncovered, until tender, about 15 minutes. Drain and let cool completely.

Rinse the saucepan and add the cooled rice and the milk to it. Place over low heat. Meanwhile, in a bowl, using a wooden spoon, beat together the egg yolks and the sugar until blended. Gradually add the egg mixture to the milk mixture, stirring constantly. Then let the mixture heat to just below a boil, continuing to stir occasionally. Remove from the heat. Stir in the raisins and vanilla, mixing gently.

Pour the rice mixture into the prepared dish. Sprinkle with the cinnamon, mace, and nutmeg. Bake until the top is golden and a knife inserted into the center comes out clean, about 45 minutes.

Serve warm or at room temperature.

Serves 6

2 cups water

Dash of salt

½ cup long-grain white rice

4 cups milk

4 egg yolks

¾ cup sugar

½ cup golden raisins

2 teaspoons vanilla extract

Ground cinnamon, ground mace, and ground nutmeg to taste

I like gingerbread, but I really think I like the smell of it baking better than I like the taste. Some people serve it with a dollop of whipped cream, but I think it's best with a spoonful of homemade applesauce. It's your choice.

Martha Washington's Gingerbread

½ cup butter, at room temperature

½ cup sugar

½ cup molasses

2 eggs

2 cups all-purpose flour

2 teaspoons baking soda

2 teaspoons baking powder

1 teaspoon ground cinnamon

1 teaspoon ground cloves

2 teaspoons ground ginger

1 cup buttermilk

Preheat an oven to 350 degrees F. Grease a 9-by-13-inch baking dish with butter.

Place the butter and sugar in a large bowl. Beat together until creamy. Stir in the molasses. Then add the eggs, one at time, beating well after each addition.

Sift together the flour, baking soda, baking powder, cinnamon, cloves, and ginger into a medium bowl. Divide the flour mixture into 3 batches. Beat the flour mixture into the butter mixture alternately with the buttermilk, beginning and ending with the flour mixture.

Pour the batter into the prepared dish. Bake until a wooden toothpick inserted into the center comes out clean, about 35 minutes. Transfer to a wire rack to cool. Serve warm or at room temperature, cut into squares.

Makes one 9-by-13-inch cake; serves 10

Martha's Sweet Tooth The English have long fancied ginger, and they carried it to the New World, where it was later tucked into the rations of American soldiers during the Revolutionary War. Martha Washington, who loved cakes and served them often at Mount Vernon, is reported to have been partial to gingerbread, a popular sweet in those days. Despite the name, this is my gingerbread recipe, although I am sure Martha would have enjoyed it.

A favorite in the South, this cake takes its name from the fact that all the ingredients are mentioned in the Bible. I have reproduced the directions here just as they appear in the recipe boxes of Southern kitchens.

Scripture Cake

Following advice in Proverbs 23:14, blend and beat well, then pour into two butter and floured cake pans and bake in a 350 degree F oven until the tops spring back to the touch. Turn out onto racks to cool.

Makes one 2-layer cake

Judges 5:25	1	cup butter
Jeremiah 6:20	2	cups sugar
Isiah 10:14	6	eggs
Genesis 24:17	1	cup water
Samuel 30:12	2	cups raisins
Samuel 30:12	2	cups dried figs
Genesis 43:11	1	cup chopped walnuts
Exodus 16:21	3	tablespoons honey
III Kings 10:2		Ground spices to taste
Leviticus 2:13	½	teaspoon salt
I Corinthians 5:6	2	teaspoon baking powder
III Kings 4:22	3 ½	cups sifted all-purpose flour

Till We Meet Again Cake Although this cake is known throughout the South as scripture cake, I call it Till We Meet Again Cake. Even after my family migrated north, South Carolina was still home, and we returned there for weddings, "big sicknesses," deaths, and always for Christmas. Each June, I went home the evening of the day school closed and left the day before school opened in September. When we made the trip by car, we packed lots of food for our journey because in those days of segregation there were few places for black travelers to eat. If we rode the train, we carried a lunch. Blacks were served in the dining car, but were forced to eat behind a partition, so Mama said considering that's how we were treated, it was just as well we didn't have the money to pay for a meal. Every time we would leave South Carolina, my Grandmama Sula would give me a hug and say, "Alright now, you member every good-bye ain't gone, every grin teeth ain't a laugh, every shut eye ain't sleep." Then she would give me a juicy kiss, slip a few coins in one hand and a few slices of this cake wrapped in waxed paper in the other, give me another juicy kiss, and say "Be good sugar, till we meet again."

The most important thing you need for this cake is a kid to lick the batter out of the bowl. If you don't have one, borrow one. You can make the cake from scratch using this recipe, or if you just want the Southern experience of filling and stacking cake layers, use a box mix for yellow cake.

Grandma Clara's Old-fashioned Jelly-filled Golden Layer Cake

Preheat an oven to 375 degrees F. Grease two 9-inch cake pans with butter and dust with flour.

In a medium bowl, sift together the flour, baking powder, salt, cinnamon, allspice, and mace.

Grate enough zest from the lemon to measure ½ teaspoon. In a large bowl, beat the butter until creamy. Add the sugar and beat until light and fluffy. Add the eggs one at a time, beating well after each addition. Stir in the vanilla and grated lemon zest.

Divide the flour mixture into 3 batches. Beat the flour mixture into the butter mixture alternately with the milk, beginning and ending with the flour mixture.

Pour the batter into the prepared pans, dividing it evenly. Bake until a cake tester inserted into the center comes out clean, about 25 minutes. Transfer to a rack to cool.

Run a knife blade around the edges of each pan to loosen the cake layers and turn the layers out of the pans. Place 1 layer on a cake plate and spread with jelly or jam. Top with the second layer and dust the top with confectioners' sugar or a sprinkling of coconut.

Makes one 9-inch cake; serves 8

2 cups sifted all-purpose flour

2 teaspoons baking powder

½ teaspoon salt

¼ teaspoon ground cinnamon

¼ teaspoon ground allspice

¼ teaspoon ground mace

1 lemon

½ cup butter, at room temperature

1 cup sugar

3 whole eggs or egg yolks

1 teaspoon vanilla extract

¾ cup milk

About ½ cup favorite jelly or jam

Confectioners' sugar or flaked dried coconut

Layer Cakes Some people call them layer cakes. Others label them stack cakes. No matter what name they go by, the idea is to spread your favorite jelly or jam between the layers. For me, that's usually grape jelly, or sometimes strawberry preserves.

I developed a crush on actor Paul Winfield after seeing him in the 1972 film Sounder, a story of black sharecroppers in the 1930s. Some time later, Josephine Premice, my upper West Side neighbor, invited me to dinner. Although Josephine's food and presentation are always extraordinary, I was very tired and was about to say I couldn't make it when she told me Paul Winfield was going to be there. Without skipping a beat, I asked, "What time is dinner?" Paul Winfield is a wonderful man and makes a wonderful bread pudding, which he has kindly consented to share here, along with a culinary tip: "The secret to this recipe is day-old cinnamon rolls, bear claws, or whatever catches your fancy at the morning bakery counter."

Paul Winfield's Bread Pudding with Cognac Sauce

2 ripe bananas

1 cup golden raisins

½ cup Cognac or cherry-flavored brandy, or as needed

1 tablespoon plus ½ cup butter

½ cup pecan pieces

1 quart milk

5 whole eggs plus 3 egg yolks

1 cup granulated sugar

1 cup heavy cream

1 teaspoon vanilla extract

1 tablespoon ground nutmeg

2 packages sweet rolls (about 12)

Peel the bananas and mash in a bowl with a fork. Transfer to a small saucepan and add the raisins and Cognac or cherry-flavored brandy just to cover. Place over medium heat and bring just to a boil. Remove from the heat, cover, and set aside.

Preheat an oven to 325 degrees F. Grease a 9-by-12-inch baking dish with about 2 teaspoons of the butter.

In a small skillet over medium-low heat, melt 1 teaspoon butter. Add the pecans and cook, stirring, for a minute or two to toast lightly. Transfer to a plate.

Put the ½ cup butter in a saucepan with the milk and place over medium heat just until small bubbles appear on the surface and the butter melts.

Meanwhile, in a large bowl, combine the whole eggs and egg yolks and the granulated sugar. Beat until smooth. Remove the milk from the heat and add the cream to it. Then slowly add the milk mixture to the egg mixture, stirring constantly. Stir in the vanilla and nutmeg.

Tear the sweet rolls into large pieces and place in the prepared baking dish. Add the raisin mixture and mix until all the ingredients are evenly distributed. Pour the milk-egg mixture over the top and sprinkle with the pecans.

Place the baking dish in a large baking pan and pour hot water into the pan to reach halfway up the sides of the dish. Bake until firm and a knife inserted into the center comes out clean, about 1 hour.

While the pudding is baking, make the sauce: Pour the milk into a small saucepan and place over medium heat just until small bubbles appear on the surface. Meanwhile, in the top pan of a double boiler, beat together the egg yolks and sugar until well mixed. Remove the milk from the heat and gradually add it to the egg mixture, stirring constantly.

Place the top pan over the lower pan of simmering water and cook, stirring occasionally, until heated through. In a small dish or cup, stir together the cornstarch and just enough water to liquefy it. Stir into the milk-yolk mixture. Cook, stirring constantly, until the mixture coats a spoon, just a few minutes.

Remove from the heat and let cool for 10 minutes, then stir in the Cognac and vanilla. (The sauce can be kept at room temperature for several hours, or it can be covered and refrigerated for up to 3 days and served cold.)

Remove the pudding from the oven. Preheat a broiler. Sift a light dusting of confectioners' sugar over the top and place under the broiler until lightly browned, just a minute or two. Remove from the oven and let the pudding cool completely.

Serve the bread pudding at room temperature with the Cognac sauce.

Serves 6 to 8

Sauce

1½ cups milk

3 eggs yolks

1 cup sugar

1 tablespoon cornstarch

About 2 tablespoons water

Cognac and vanilla extract to taste

Confectioners' sugar

I'm the mommy in this case, and I bake only drop-topped cobblers. I don't roll nothing but my eyes, which means making cobblers is easy.

Mommy's Quick Drop Peach Cobbler

1 ½ to 2 pounds peaches

⅔ cup brown sugar

2 cups Bisquick

2 tablespoons butter

Granulated sugar

Preheat an oven to 350 degrees F.

Peel, halve, and pit the peaches, then slice; you will need 3 cups.

In a heavy saucepan over medium-low heat, combine the peaches and brown sugar. Bring just to a boil, stirring often and making sure the peaches and sugar don't scorch. Remove from the heat and set aside to cool.

Using the 2 cups Bisquick, follow the instructions for making biscuits on the Bisquick box. Pour the peaches into a 9-by-13-inch baking dish, spreading them evenly. Drop the Bisquick batter by tablespoonfuls on top of the fruit, covering the entire surface.

Cut the butter into bits and dot the top. Sprinkle with granulated sugar. Bake until the crust is golden and crisp, about 30 minutes. Serve warm or at room temperature.

Serves 8

There is a Gullah expression, "You are a huckleberry beyond my persimmon." I love it. I am not sure what it means, but I love it, use it often and it was the inspiration for a song I wrote for Nyam, my food folk opera. This cobbler is traditionally made with huckleberries, but since they are wild and usually the only people lucky enough to have some on hand are foragers, I have used blueberries, which are similar in appearance. But if you can get your hands on some real huckleberries, use them. Sometimes in the summer, you can find huckleberries stocked in produce markets in the South, as well as the Northeast and Northwest.

Blueberry or Huckleberry Honey Cobbler

1 egg

⅓ cup milk

1½ cups yellow cornmeal

1 teaspoon baking powder

1 teaspoon salt

½ cup honey

2 quarts blueberries

3 tablespoons butter

Preheat an oven to 350 degrees F. Grease a 9-by-13-inch baking dish with butter.

In a bowl, lightly beat the egg until blended, then beat in the milk, cornmeal, baking powder, salt, and ¼ cup of the honey, mixing well.

Place the berries in the bottom of the prepared dish, spreading them evenly. Pour the remaining ¼ cup honey over the berries. Then, using a tablespoon, drop the batter by spoonfuls onto the berries, covering the surface of the dish evenly.

Cut the butter into bits and use to dot the surface. Bake until the crust is golden, about 30 minutes. Serve warm or at room temperature.

Serves 8

About Huckleberries Lots of people think that huckleberries and blueberries are the same thing, with the only difference being that the former are wild and the latter are cultivated. But they don't even belong to the same genus. The term huckleberry is used for a number of wild blue and black berries that are native to the United States and are members of the Gaylussacia genus. Each berry contains ten large seeds and is considerably tarter than its lookalike distant cousin, the blueberry, a member of the Vaccinium genus.

I don't have the patience for making pie crusts, so I always buy a good-quality premade one at the market. If you have a favorite crust recipe, use it here. I've tried a number of different varieties of sweet potatoes in this pie, with flesh from deep yellow to ivory, and it always turns out delicious. Just don't mix your colors in one pie.

No-Fail Sweet Potato Pie

Scrub the sweet potatoes but do not peel. Bring a large saucepan of water to a boil. Add the sweet potatoes and boil until tender when pierced with a fork, 30 to 40 minutes; the timing will depend on the size of the sweet potatoes. Drain well, let cool, and peel. Place the sweet potatoes in a bowl and mash with a potato masher until no lumps remain. Measure out 2 cups; reserve the remainder for another use.

Preheat an oven to 350 degrees F.

In a large bowl, beat the eggs until blended. Add the 2 cups mashed sweet potatoes and beat well. Stir in the milk until well mixed, then gradually beat in the sugar, nutmeg, cinnamon, allspice, and salt. Add the vanilla and stir well. Taste and adjust with a little more spice, if you like.

Pour the sweet potato mixture into the pie crust. Bake until the center is firm and a knife inserted into the center comes out clean, about 45 minutes. Transfer to a rack and let cool before serving.

Makes one 10-inch pie; serves 6 to 8

3 sweet potatoes

3 eggs

½ cup evaporated milk

½ cup sugar

½ teaspoon ground nutmeg

½ teaspoon ground cinnamon

½ teaspoon ground allspice'

Dash of salt

1 teaspoon vanilla extract

1 store-bought ready-to-bake 10-inch pie crust

Sweet Potato Pie I've tasted a lot of sweet potato pies, served up everywhere from family tables to church suppers to five-star restaurants. Reputations are made and broken over this legendary dessert. And the best sweet potato pie maker I know is my friend artist Kenneth Brown. Kenneth's pie is famous in New York, and he makes it from a time-honored family recipe that originated in the Georgia Sea Islands. But whenever I ask him for the recipe, he seems to suffer from memory loss. Therefore, I have used my own family recipe, and I consider it pretty good competition.

I am using pears for the sauce here, but you can use ripe peaches, nectarines, or whatever fruit you might choose, pairing it with its matching nectar. Or you might add a little rum in place of some of the nectar.

Watermelon Wedges with Blueberries & Pear Sauce

Pear sauce

2 ripe pears

¼ cup pear nectar

4 watermelon wedges, each 2 to 3 inches wide

1 cup blueberries

To make the sauce, halve, core, and peel the pears. Cut into large pieces and place in a blender or in a food processor fitted with the metal blade. Add the pear nectar and process until smooth, about 1 minute.

Place a watermelon on each of 4 individual plates. Spoon ¼ cup of the blueberries over each wedge. Drizzle the pear sauce over the top, dividing it evenly.

Serves 4

Thirst Quencher Watermelon first grew in the middle of Africa's great Kalahari Desert, where it was plucked from its vine and enjoyed for its watery contents by thirsty traders en route to distant markets. Those travelers knew what they were doing, for watermelons are about 90 percent water. They are also high in potassium and vitamins A and C, and for those watching their weight, very low in calories.

use your imagination to create a variety of fruit kabobs. For example, if you can find watermelons with different colors of flesh, thread the multicolored cubes onto skewers alternately with grapes. The kabobs are great cooked over hot coals, but a broiler is a good alternative. They not only make an unusual dessert, but are also wonderful as a side dish to grilled meats.

Mixed-Fruit Kabobs

1 small pineapple

1 piece watermelon, about 1½ pounds

4 bananas

¼ cup Cointreau or other orange-flavored liqueur

Soak 8 bamboo skewers in water to cover.

Using a sharp knife, trim away the peel from the pineapple, then cut the pineapple crosswise into 1-inch-thick slices. Cut the core out of the center of each slice. Cut the slices into 1-inch cubes.

Cut the rind off the watermelon and pick over and discard any seeds. Cut the flesh into 1-inch cubes.

Peel the bananas and cut them into 1-inch cubes.

Drain the skewers and thread the pineapple, melon, and banana cubes onto them, alternating the fruits. Place the loaded skewers on a platter and brush the fruits on all sides with the liqueur. Marinate for 30 minutes.

Meanwhile, prepare a fire in a charcoal grill or preheat a broiler.

Place the skewers on the grill rack or on a broiler pan and cook, turning as needed to prevent burning, until lightly browned and hot throughout, about 5 minutes. Serve immediately.

Serves 8

Watermelon Contests Numerous watermelon festivals are held around the united States every year. One of the most popular events at these festivities is the watermelon-seed spitting contest. To date, the world record for seed spitting is 66 feet 11 inches. That's certainly better that I could ever do.

Don't feel limited to this list of ingredients. This punch can be made with an endless variety of nectars and juices. What I am giving you here is simply a favorite of mine.

Desserts & More **177**

Calypso Punch

Make sure all the juices are well chilled. In a large pitcher, combine them and stir to mix well.

Peel the mango(es) and cut the pulp away from the large pit(s). Place the pulp in a blender and puree until smooth.

Add the mango puree to the juices and stir well. Then add enough crushed ice to keep the juices nicely chilled. Add enough grenadine syrup to give the mixture a pleasant pomegranate tartness. Mix well.

Serve immediately in tall glasses.

1 part papaya juice

1 part passion fruit juice

1 part orange juice

1 part guava juice

1 mango per quart of mixed juices

Crushed ice

Grenadine syrup to taste

My Aunt Zip always had a jar of this lemonade in her icebox, and I mean a jar! She was into recycling before it was the thing to do. This recipe will satisfy thirst all summer and all winter.

Aunt Zipporah's Spicy Boiled Lemonade

6 lemons

6 cups water

2 cups sugar

1 teaspoon whole cloves

Crushed ice

Halve all the lemons and squeeze the juice from them. Strain through a fine-mesh sieve into a large nonaluminum saucepan.

Add the water, sugar, and cloves. Place over low heat and bring to a boil, stirring constantly. As soon as the mixture has reached a boil and the sugar is completely dissolved, remove from the heat and let cool completely. Remove and discard the cloves, then chill the lemonade.

Serve the lemonade over crushed ice in tall glasses.

Serves 6

Aunt Zipporah My Aunt Zipporah never owned a cookbook. She loved to talk about food, and was a living keeper of the family's culinary records. She knew precisely how much a pinch was and how little a dash was. She could tell when to stir and when to leave the pot closed. And she was full of kitchen wisdom and sound proverbs like "We can all hide the smoke, but what you goin' to do with the fire?"

The Southern beverage of choice. It's the year-round, every-meal drink. And in between meals, too. In the South, you get free refills on iced tea in restaurants. ("Do you want your tea sweetened or unsweetened, Sugar?") In the North, refills are generally extra.

Grandma Clara's Southern Iced Tea Classic

Bring the water to a boil. Place the tea bags in a heatproof gallon jar and pour the boiling water over them. (If you don't have a gallon jar, use 2 or 3 smaller jars, dividing the tea bags and sugar evenly among them.)

Add the sugar, stir to dissolve, cover, and allow to steep for 10 to 15 minutes, or to your taste. Remember, you will probably be serving the tea in a glassful of ice, so it should be fairly strong, as the ice will melt and dilute it. Let the tea cool.

Slice the lemons and add to the tea. Cover and refrigerate. Enjoy on any day.

Makes 1 gallon

1 gallon water

6 Lipton tea bags

2 cups sugar

2 lemons

Iced Tea Memories Grandma Clara is my mother, and she always kept iced tea in a pretty Art Deco pitcher – a piece of tin foil wrapped over the spout to protect it from outside odors – in her icebox, and later in her refrigerator. Her iced tea was so good that you always wanted to suck on the lemon slices to get the last bit of flavor. And she doted on Lipton's.

THE AMERICAS'
FAMILY KITCHEN™

SHOW 101
CAROLINA GOLD
From the early 1700's to the Civil War, the Carolina Coast was teemingwith beautiful golden rice plantations. In that region, rice became known as "Carolina Gold." Vertamae demonstrates how to cook fluffy and flavorful Gullahrice perfectly every time as she showcases one of the most important food staples known to humankind, a nourishing grain that is eaten at breakfast, lunch and dinner all around the world.

Proper Gullah Rice
Classic Red Rice
White and Wild Rice Salad
Oven-Baked Gullah Veggie Paella
Old-Timey Rice Pudding
Wild Rice and Mushroom Pilaf
Lentil Soup Topped with Chopped Parsley and Cilantro

SHOW 102
PORGY, BASS & CATFISH BARKING
In ancient Nigeria, the catfish was a royal symbol for peace, prosperity and fertility. To many Africans, catfish (or "mudfish" as they called it), had mythical qualities. Today, catfish farming is a big industry, especially in the Southern U.S. states of Mississippi and Louisiana. Vertamae prepares a host of catfish dishes and gives viewers the inside story on the great watermen who made up the legendary Mosquito Fleets; the real story behind Porgy of "Porgy and Bess" fame; Catfish Row; and how to tell if a fish is fresh.

Mullet Stew
Fried Catfish
Boiled Cod Steaks
Oven-Baked Porgies
Grits
Hush Puppies
Baked Bass in Foil with Vegetables

SHOW 103
BRAZIL
Many countries have flavored the melting pot of Brazil, helping to create a rich, diverse and delicious food culture. Throughout Brazilian cuisine, from the national dish Feijoada (black beans simmered in smoked pork meats) to Churrasco (barbecued meats and fish), the Afro-Brazilian flavors are eminent. Vertamae takes viewers on a tour of Brazil's culinary background, traveling fromRio to Bahia.

Bahian Shrimp Stew
Brazilian Black Beans
Palm Hearts and Beet Salad
Okra with Cilantro
Collard Greens Brazilian Style
Peanut Candy
Manioc Meal
Palm Heart Soup

SHOW 104
GOOBERS
Exchanging and duplicating crop cultivation between Africa and the Americas has continued from ancient times until today. Goobers, best known as peanuts, most likely came to Africa from Brazil via Portuguese slave traders around 1500. In the early 1900's, Dr. George Washington Carver, a noted research scientist from Tuskegee University, published a cookbook of 125 peanut recipes to "show the possibilities of the peanut." Before his death in 1943, Carver had developed 300 uses for peanuts, Including a massage oil to help the recovery of polio victims. Vertamae salutes the accomplishments of Dr. Carver as she cooks a number of recipes with peanuts.

Peanut Salsa
Groundnut Stew

Spinach and Goobers
Shrimp and Goobers
Apple, Peanut and Vegetable
Salad
Dr. George Washington Carver's
Peanuts Baked with Rice

SHOW 105
BARBECUE

Cooking over open fire is one of the oldest known cooking methods. Bobby Seale, author of *Barbeque'n with Bobby* joins Vertamae as guest pit master to prepare a down-home barbecue feast. Viewers learn the secret to preparing the perfect barbecue, along with tips on starting the pit fire, pit basting, and the difference between long, slow, smokey barbecuing and fast grilling.

Jerked Chicken
Cole Slaw
Beef Brisket
Pasta and Bean Salad
Bobby Seale's Smoked Spicy-
Hot Barbeque Chicken

SHOW 106
HOPPING JOHN

There are many versions of the tale of how the dish "Hopping John" got its name, including one that claimed children would hop around the table in anticipation of eating it. Hopping John, a traditional dish of rice and beans —is also known by many different names. In Jamaica, it's called "rice and pigeon peas;" in Cuba, it's called "the Moors and the Christians;" and in New Orleans, it's called "red beans and rice."

Traditionally served on New Year's Day, Hopping John is believed to bring good luck in the coming year.

Hopping John with Sausage and
Blackeyed Peas
Limping Susan with Okra, Rice
and Shrimp
Cuban Classic Black Beans and
Rice
Hopping John with Cow Peas and
Hamhocks

SHOW 107
YAMS

What's the difference between a yam and a sweet potato? The history of this versatile vegetable is as extensive as its great nutritional value. Although the words have become interchangeable in the United States, only "sweet potatoes" are grown in the United States, while "yams" are cultivated in tropical places like South America and Africa. The word "yam" itself is derived from the West African root word "nyam," which means, "to eat."

Sweet Potato Pie
Oven Fried Yams
Sweet Potato Pone
Mashed Sweet Potatoes
French Fried Yams
Mama Rosa's Gingered Yam and
Apple Bake

SHOW 108
AMERICAN CREOLE

The culinary terrain of the Atlantic Coast is one of the most diverse in the United States. Perhaps nowhere else in the country is the food so mixed. A new world of fusion cooking is on the front burner — Cuban sandwiches, empanadas and dishes native to the Middle East can be found in restaurants and homes up and down the coast, along with gumbo and jambalaya — this blending is what makes up Creole. Back in The Americas' Family Kitchen, Vertamae shares some Creole cooking history as she prepares a variety of Creole dishes.

Tomatoes and Okra
Vegetable Gumbo
Shrimp and Okra Gumbo
Arroz Con Pollo (rice and chicken)
New Orleans Washday Red
Beans
Chicken Creole
Jambalaya

SHOW 109
WATERMELON

One of the oldest fruits known to humankind, watermelons first grew in the middle of the Kalahari Desert. There they became a source of water for thirsty traders who later began to sell the seeds in cities along the ancient Mediterranean trade routes. Watermelons were brought to North America by European colonists and African slaves, and, today, there are more than 200 varieties grown in 44 states. Marchel'le Barber, owner of Martha's Crib, a multi-cultural arts and craft store, shows Vertamae some artifacts she has collected that historically perpetuates the

negative stereotypes of African-Americans and watermelon.
Watermelon Soup
Three Melon Salad
Broiled Fruit Kabobs
Watermelon Slush
Watermelon Wedges with Blueberries and Pear Sauce

SHOW 110
BATTER EXPRESS

The "Batter Express" is a plantation term for the path leading from the cook house to the big house. Paying tribute to the women who stood in the heat of the cook house for over two centuries, Vertamae cooks up a few of the "old-timey" plantation recipes that are still eaten today. As she prepares these dishes, Vertamae shares a few enlightening tales about the cooks who served George Washington and Thomas Jefferson, the origins of the hoe cake, and the history behind the secret gardens of the slaves.

Monticello Macaroni and Cheese
Braised Guinea Hen
Martha Washington's Gingerbread
Secret Garden Mixed Greens with Smoked Turkey Wings

SHOW 111
CARIBBEAN CREOLE

If the word "creole" makes you think of Louisiana, The Americas' Family Kitchen is about to expand your culinary horizons. Extending far beyond the bounds of the Louisiana state border, the food and people called "creole" are actually a blend of Native American, African, European, Indian, and Asian cultures. Vertamae blends cilantro, chives, cinnamon, vanilla and, of course, the creole seasoning of choice, pepper, to create a number of delicious Caribbean dishes.

Jamaican Curried Goat
Saltfish Fritters
Sunshine Soup
Ackee and Salt Fish
Rice and Gungu Peas
Caribbean Shrimp and Okra Gumbo
Calypso Punch

SHOW 112
CORNY, CORNY, CORN

The only truly indigenous American grain, corn was the cornerstone in the ancient civilizations of the Americas. This Native American gift, often referred to as "maize," became one of the first crops exported from the New World into West Africa. Corn eventually became a "poor man's staple" the world over because of its amazing adaptability to other climates, and its inexpensive cultivation. Today, whether served on the cob, in a stew, or popped, corn remains a popular food within the Americas and around the world.

Fungi
Low Country Boil
Corn/Shrimp Chowder
Native American/African

American Cobbler
Albuquerque Blue Corn Bread
Succotash

SHOW 113
SUNDAY SUPPERS

The old tradition of family and friends sharing a Sunday meal together is making a comeback across the United States. Vertamae invites viewers to pull up a chair as she and her grandchildren prepare a sumptuous, stress-free Sunday supper in The Americas' Family Kitchen. Although the menu is old fashioned Southern, Vertamae tailors these recipes for the 90's taste.

Black-Eyed Pea Salad
Candied Yams
Cornbread
Collard Greens
Lemony Oven-Fried Chicken Wings
Oscar Brown Sugar Cookies

Index

Mail Order Sources

Here is a partial list of mail order sources for Southern foods. Many have a catalogs, available upon request, that offer a wide range of products.

A & W Island Food Store
2634 San Pablo Avenue
Berkeley, CA 94702
(510) 649-9195
(African yams, plantains, salted mackerel, pigeon peas, Caribbean spices)

Adams Milling Company
Route 6, Box 148A
Dothan, Alabama 36303
(800) 239-4233
(Grits milled from whole kernel corn and other corn products, such as water-ground cornmeal)

Bassie's Choice
P. O. Box 1
Smithfield, Virginia 23431
(800) 292-2773
(Smithfield hams, Williamsburg slab bacon)

Battistella's Seafood, Inc.
910 Touro Street
New Orleans, LA 70166
(504) 949-2724
(Live crawfish, catfish, crab products)

Casa Hispañia, International
73 Poningo Street
Port Chester, NY 10578
(914) 939-9333
(Central and South American ingredients)

Chattanooga Bakery
P. O. Box 111
Chattanooga, Tennessee 37401
(800) 251-3404
(Moon pies)

The Company Store
1039 Decatur Street
New Orleans, Louisiana 70116
(800) 772-2927
(Café de Monde coffee, beignet mix, spices, cookbooks)

DeKalb World Farmer's Market
3000 East Ponce de Leon
Decatur, GA 30034
(404) 377-6401
(Fresh seasonal produce, Caribbean seasonings, dried shrimp)

Exclusively Barbecue
P. O. Box 3048
Concord, North Carolina 28025
(800) 948-1009
(Barbecue sauces, grills and apparel)

Hoppin' John's
30 Pinckney Street
Charleston, South Carolina 299401
(803) 577-6404
(Stone-ground cornmeal, corn flour)

International Market
365 Somerville Avenue
Somerville, MA 02143
(800) 455-1880
(Dendé oil, cassava meal, coconut milk)

Konriko Company Store
307 Ann Street
New Iberta, IA 70562
(800) 551-3245
(Louisiana rice, Creole seasonings, bases for gumbo, crawfish boil)

Pickwick Catfish Farm
4155 Highway 57
Counce, Tennessee 38326
(901) 689-3805
(Smoked catfish)

Sunny Caribe
216 King Street
Charleston, SC 29401
(803) 723-6957
(Jerk seasonings, hot sauce, curry blends, ginger syrup)

Sunnyland Farms
P. O. Box 8200
Albany, Georgia 31706-8200
(912) 883-3085
(Pecans, fruits, candies)

Trappey's Fine Foods, Inc.
c/o McIlhenny Company
Avery Island, Louisiana 70513
(800) 634-9599
(Hot sauces)

W. B. Rodenberry Co, Inc.
P. O. Box 60
Cairo, GA 31728
(912) 377-1431
(Boiled peanuts)

There is an African saying that it takes a whole village to raise one child. Well, it takes a community of many professionals to produce a television show. The production of *The Americas' Family Kithchen with Vertamae Grosvenor*, the television series, was a concerted effort by many talented people. Our series reflects the blending of African, European and Native American foodways, music and culture. Our production team worked in the spirit of that blending, and contributed generously of their creativity to make it all work.

First and foremost, I want to thank Vertamae for her talent and creativity. I especially want to thank Bill McCarter, President and CEO of Window To The World Communications, Inc., Bob Mauro, Senior V. P. of The Chicago Production Center, Katherine Lauderdale, Senior V. P., New Ventures, and Ron Nigro, Director, New Ventures, for their support.

I extend my heartfelt thanks to the entire production team and to those individuals and companies who donated their time, talent, furnishings and equipment in support of *The Americas' Family Kithchen with Vertamae Grosvenor.* It has been a joyful and divine pleasure working with all of you.

Production Staff

Beverly Price	Producer
Tim Ward	Director
Kathy Giangreco	Segment Producer
Cynthia Malek	Associate Director
Michael Loewenstein	Scenic Design
David Tennenbaum	Assistant Scenic Design
Carol A. Sanders	Art Direction
Cindy McCullough	Graphic Design
Steve Workman	Series Attorney
Tracye Campbell	Production Assistant
April Davis	Production Assistant
Colleen Dougherty	Production Assistant
Aimee Tolson	Makeup
Conchita Rodriguez	Production Intern
Vicky De Guia	Production Accountant

Kitchen Staff

Sylvia Anderson	Kitchen Staff
Maria Baez Kijac	Kitchen Staff
Norman Womack	Kitchen Staff

Supporters

WOOD-MODE Fine Custom Cabinetry
Don Outlet Stores Chicago
Varig Airlines
Whirlpool
Chantal Cookware Corp.
Kitchen Aid
Kohler Co.
Marshall Field's

Special Thanks to:

Ann Ponce
David Csicsko
James Fox
Barbara Samuels
Design Imports India
Portal Publications
Swahili Imports, Inc.
Americaware
Waechtersbach
OGGI Corp.

Studio /Post Production Staff

Tim Snell	Production Manager
Jim Lindberg	Camera
Steve Miller	Camera
Carlos Tronshaw	Camera
Roy D. Alan	Camera
Emmett E. Wilson	Camera
Richard J. Well	Technical Director
Jim Gedwellas	Lighting Director
Rick Moyer	Lighting Assistant
John Kennamer	Audio
Jim Mancini	Audio
Marvin J. Pienta	Floor Director
Bruce Rehberger	Floor Director
William Alvelo	Floor Director
Barbara E. Allen	Tape
Ricky Wells	Tape
Kim R. Breitenbach	Floor Assistant
Maurice Smith	Floor Assistant
Rex Allen Victor	Floor Assistant
John Oppy	Video
Tim Boyd	Video
Tom Siegel	Off-line Editor
Don De Martini	On-line Editor
Timothy H. Jackson	On-line Editor
Paul Thornton	On-line Editor
Jerry Binder	On-line audio
Robert Dove	On-line audio
Jim Guthrie	On-line audio
Barbara Shintani	Electronic titles

FRANCES J. HARTH
Executive Producer
Chicago 1996

About Vertamae Grosvenor

Storyteller, poet, and culinary anthropologist Vertamae Grosvenor has been exploring and sharing the roots of culinary culture for more than 25 years. From her 1970 autobiographical cookbook, *Vibration Cooking or the Travel Notes of a Geechee Girl*, to her 1996 James Beard Award for *Seasonings*, she has always known that stories are half the pleasure of good food.

As a National Public Radio Correspondent, Grosvenor contributes regular features on African-American creativity and community to NPR newsmagazines. From 1988 until 1995 she hosted NPR's award-winning documentary series *Horizons*, for which she had long been producing stories. Her documentary "Never Enough Too Soon," about South Carolina's Daufuskie Island, earned her a Robert F. Kennedy and an Ohio State Award. She had a featured role in *Daughters of the Dust*.

Seasonings, her radio specials on holiday cuisines, was named Best Radio Food Series by the James Beard Awards in 1996. She has also been honored by the National Association of Black Journalists and by the DuPont-Columbia Awards, among many others.

Grosvenor learned to cook in the South Carolina low country, where the people and the language are interchangeably called Geechee or Gullah. Indeed she drew on this background when she served as consultant and writer for National Geographic's Gullah documentary. Her career has consistently circled back to an exploration of how food carries culture through different venues, acquiring new flavors and traditions along the way.

Grosvenor has been a Contributing Editor to *Essence* and *Elan Magazines* and has written for the *New York Times*, *The Village Voice*, *The Washington Post*, *Redbook*, and *Ebony*. She was a space goddess with *Sun Ra Solar Arkestra*. She has performed her "food folk opera" *Nyam* (Gullah for "eat") in numerous locales around the country.

Grosvenor lives in Washington, D.C., where she enjoys the city's rich mix of cultures and cuisines, and the presence of several grandchildren.